British Bu
Since 1950
Trendsetting Designs

GAVIN BOOTH

BRITAIN'S BUSES SERIES, VOLUME 10

Front cover image: The Dennis Dart, typically with Plaxton Pointer bodywork, brought affordable low-floor buses to Britain. This Stagecoach in Cumbria bus picks up passengers in Carlisle in 2008.

Back cover image: As new bus deliveries move towards zero emission standards, hydrogen fuel-cell buses have joined several UK fleets. This is one of the earliest double-deckers, a Metroline Wrights Hydroliner, in London service in 2021.

Title page image: The first fleet of articulated single-deckers to enter service in the UK were used in South Yorkshire. This Leyland/DAB example is in Sheffield in 1994, in the company of other significant types covered in this book – Dennis Dominators, Daimler Fleetlines and Leyland Nationals.

Contents page image: The Dennis Trident was a successful early low-floor double-deck model. This Stagecoach Busways Trident with Alexander ALX400 bodywork is in Newcastle in 2000.

Published by Key Books
An imprint of Key Publishing Ltd
PO Box 100
Stamford
Lincs PE19 1XQ

www.keypublishing.com

The rights of Gavin Booth to be identified as the author of this book has been asserted in accordance with the Copyright, Designs and Patents Act 1988 Sections 77 and 78.

Copyright © Gavin Booth, 2022

ISBN 978 1 80282 240 3

Typeset by SJmagic DESIGN SERVICES, India.

Contents

Introduction

Countless thousands of buses have been bought by UK operators over the past century. Some have been supremely successful while others have been duds, and in between were the buses that carried out their daily task of taking passengers where they wanted to go, relatively quietly and without any drama.

Some are remembered because they broke the mould, because they challenged existing norms and took bus design and technology into fresh areas, often with great success – but not always. Occasionally, the realisation came that this mould-breaking design was not what the industry wanted, even after millions of pounds had been spent in development.

Looking back, it is tempting to surmise that bus manufacturers did not always take much account of what their customers were looking for. Even the major builders misjudged the market from time to time, producing models that nobody really wanted. Or perhaps models that only one particularly vocal, and potentially valuable, customer wanted.

So, there have been some duds. Some brave duds, it must be said – ones that misread the market, were painfully unreliable, or that were built to meet the requirements of specific operators. Not too many, fortunately, but some are included in this book to remind us of innovative ideas that just may not have been right for the time.

It tended to be the major players among the bus builders that had the research facilities and the financial resources to float new ideas and, while they may not always have hit the target, they were usually prepared to rush back to the drawing board and learn from their mistakes.

I am grateful to the photographers who provided images to plug a few gaps – Keith McGillivray, Sholto Thomas and Tony Wilson. Their photos are credited, and the remainder are mine or from my collection. And for period flavour, I have included examples of contemporary advertising.

Gavin Booth
Edinburgh

The Leyland Atlantean started the move to rear-engined buses in the UK. Against a gathering sky in 1992 is a VFM Buses Roe-bodied 1983 delivery, along with a Northern General 1983 Leyland National 2 – both important ground-breaking models. VFM (Value For Money) was a Northern General local brand.

Chapter 1

Who bought the buses?

It tended to be the larger operators that had the greatest influence on the design and development of new buses – the customers with the greatest spending power. The bus bosses would be courted by the manufacturers' sales director, wined and dined and rewarded with buses that suited their needs. It was left to the regional sales managers to call on the fleet engineers at bus companies further down the pecking order to try to persuade them that the answer to all their needs was in the sales catalogue, and preferably as near to the standard offering as possible.

London, the major cities and the big groups had the requirements for most new buses. London Transport, under its varying guises, had huge buying power but was very specific about the buses it needed – until it seemed to lose its way in the 1960s and invested heavily in buses that were not apparently ideal for the capital's requirements and were sold off very quickly until a new generation of buses, often designed with London orders in mind, came along in the 1970s. After the sell-off of the business units of London Buses in the mid-1990s, the successful franchise holders bought what were essentially off-the-shelf models with bodywork that was tweaked to an agreed London standard. And then, of course, in the 2010s came the 1,000-strong New Bus for London fleet, alias the New Routemaster – but still the Borismaster to many of us.

There were 95 municipal operators in 1968, ranging in size from Colwyn Bay with just five buses to Birmingham with over 1,500. They each had their own ideas about vehicle types and specifications and often had preferred suppliers. All of that changed between 1969 and 1974, when more than 30 of the municipal bus operators were swept up into the newly formed Passenger Transport Executives (PTEs).

London Transport, with by far the largest bus fleet in the UK, had a long tradition of designing and specifying the buses used on its services. Two of the fleet of 4,825 AEC Regent RT types taken into stock between 1939 and 1954 were still featuring in AEC advertising in 1952, under the title 'Proud Association'.

Fifty years later and Transport for London returned to designing its own double-deck model, the New Routemaster, built by Wrights in Ballymena. Boris Johnson, then Mayor of London, drives one of the first production examples out of the Ballymena plant at its launch in 2004. There were 1,000 buses of this type produced.

At one time, municipal operators included a small proportion of single-deckers in what were predominantly double-deck fleets. This is a 1962 Colchester Corporation AEC Reliance with Weymann 45-seat body in 1974, acquired from Salford Corporation and typical of the underfloor-engined buses delivered in the 1950s and 1960s.

Municipal operators were often loyal to local builders to support local employers. These two Lancashire-built Blackburn Corporation Leyland Atlantean AN68s, dating from 1979 and 1983, had 74-seat bodies built by East Lancs in Blackburn. The 1979 bus, on the right, is celebrating 50 years of Blackburn buses.

The new PTEs inherited a combined, and often very mixed, fleet of over 10,000 buses, and the PTEs quickly developed standard models, which were bought in substantial numbers in the 1970s and 1980s, until the privatisation process between 1988 and 1994 saw the conurbations served by companies belonging to new groups that had emerged in the wake of privatisation, and which had their own ideas about bus design.

Above left: The creation of Passenger Transport Executives (PTEs) from 1969 meant that many municipal bus fleets were subsumed into these new authorities. Selnec (South-East Lancashire, North-East Cheshire) quickly set about replacing a very mixed inheritance of buses with new standard types and built up a large fleet of new buses to this basic design – Daimler Fleetline and Leyland Atlantean chassis with Northern Counties and Park Royal bodies – between 1972 and 1982. This is a 1973 Fleetline/Park Royal 75-seater in Manchester in 1979.

Above right: West Midlands PTE also supported local industry, first with Metro-Cammell-bodied Daimler Fleetlines and then with Metro-Cammell-Weymann (MCW) Metrobuses. This 1984 73-seat Mk2 version is on the experimental guided busway at Short Heath, Birmingham, in 1986.

Above: Merseyside PTE built up a large fleet of Alexander-bodied Leyland Atlantean AN68s between 1972 and 1984. This newly delivered example is at Liverpool's Pier Head in 1984.

Left: The West Yorkshire PTE bought different double-deck models, including Roe-bodied Leyland Olympian 76-seaters, like this 1983 example in Leeds in 2004, following the privatisation of the PTE and acquisition by FirstBus.

South Yorkshire PTE (SYPTE) favoured the Dennis Dominator with Alexander bodywork, like this 1984 78-seat example in Sheffield in 2001, in the First Mainline fleet following privatisation of the PTE.

Two bus groups dominated the non-municipal bus industry in England and Wales throughout the 1950s and 1960s. These were the British Electric Traction (BET) Group and the Tilling Group – from 1963, the Transport Holding Company (THC). They were two very different animals. The BET Group was privately owned and controlled over 10,000 buses, often in busy urban areas, and while a recognisable breed of BET single-deck bus emerged in the 1950s and 1960s, there did appear to be some leeway in terms of the chassis and bodywork that the companies could choose. This was particularly evident in the double-deck fleet, where companies like Ribble and Southdown were allowed to develop instantly recognisable models.

No such luxury for the Tilling Group, which had passed into state control under the British Transport Commission (BTC) in 1948, and which, in 1968, comprised some 30 companies in England and Wales running nearly 10,000 buses, as well as in-house bus manufacturing facilities in the shape of Bristol and Eastern Coach Works (ECW). With very few exceptions, between 1948 and 1965, Tilling companies were required to choose only Bristol/ECW products, and these were not available to operators that did not come under the state-owned umbrella. A range of models was provided, designed in conjunction with company managers, where prototypes were tested in service to iron

Above left: The BET Group companies had some freedom in the buses they bought, but a distinct BET single-deck style was evident in its single-deckers for many years. Duple made the debatable claim in this 1969 advert that this 11m (36ft)-long Willowbrook-bodied Leyland Leopard for Maidstone & District was 'Britain's finest public service vehicle'. Buses to this general design were built by various bodybuilders for BET and other UK fleets.

Above right: Uniquely in the BET Group, the giant Midland Red company had been building buses to its own design for many years, but, in this 1963 advert, Daimler is proudly trumpeting that it has won an order for 50 Fleetlines, with bodywork by Alexander. Gradually, more off-the-peg models joined the Midland Red fleet.

The state-owned Tilling Group companies had a restricted choice of models, designed and built for them by the state-owned Bristol and Eastern Coach Works (ECW) companies. This 1956 underfloor-engined Bristol LS5G with 45-seat ECW body for United Automobile Services is typical of many supplied in the 1950s.

out any problems. The best-known outcomes of this situation are probably the Bristol Lodekka, the ground-breaking low-height double-decker, and the Bristol RE, widely regarded as the best of the 1960s rear-engined single-deck buses.

When the THC companies in England and Wales merged with the BET group in 1969 to create the National Bus Company, there was clearly scope to create a more standardised fleet, with vehicle choices controlled from the centre. So, in a few short years, the number of municipal and company operators making vehicle choices had declined from 163 to just the remaining 62 municipalities, the seven PTEs and National Bus. This had the inevitable knock-on effect on the manufacturing industry, which, through acquisitions, was narrowing down to just one dominant player – Leyland.

Bristol/ECW double-deckers included the K types and the ground-breaking Lodekka, and when rear-engined models were required, it developed the VRT. The great majority had ECW bodies, like the bus in the background of this 1978 view, but East Kent also received Willowbrook-bodied examples, like this 74-seater when new in 1978. Both buses wear National Bus Company's (NBC) standard poppy red/white livery style.

The standard NBC single-deck model was the integral Leyland National model, built on a production line at Workington. This typical Mk1 National, a 49-seater, is at Norwich's undulating bus station in 1979, with Bristol/ECW VRT double-deckers in the background.

The Scottish Bus Group (SBG), state-owned since 1949 and running nearly 5,000 buses in 1968, had the advantage that it could buy its buses on the open market, as well as placing an agreed proportion of its annual orders with Bristol and ECW. However, there were other operators outside the THC that might well have bought the Lodekka or the RE but were denied access to Bristol and ECW models until 1965. As soon as the RE became available on the open market, it gained valuable new customers.

In the early years of the 20th century, the UK bus manufacturing industry had taken some time to find its feet and adapt to the growth of the bus industry, particularly following World War One, when

Scottish Bus Group (SBG) could buy Bristol/ECW models, as well as shopping on the open market. This 1981 Dennis Dominator with low-height Alexander 79-seat body is in East Kilbride when new.

Although Alexander-bodied Leyland Leopards were popular with some SBG fleets, there was a demand from some group companies for Gardner underfloor-engined single-deck chassis. The Seddon Pennine 7 was developed for the group and two Eastern Scottish Alexander-bodied examples are in Galashiels depot in 1982 – a newly delivered Y type 53-seat bus on the left and a 1979 T type dual-purpose 49-seater on the right. Dual-purpose types, at home on longer-distance routes and on coaching duties, were popular with SBG and the other major groups.

there emerged a greater distinction between chassis built for goods and for passenger use. The industry grew up very quickly in the 1920s, as buses became lower-built with more sophisticated mechanical components and pneumatic, rather than solid, tyres. Four of the longest surviving bus manufacturers had their roots in the years before World War One – Dennis in 1895, Leyland in 1896, Daimler in 1904 and AEC (Associated Equipment Company) in 1912. Many others came and went, and though it seemed likely that the bus builders that had managed to survive into the 1970s might still be around in UK ownership beyond the 1980s, only Dennis still remains, though now as part of a North American business, the NFI Group.

It is easy to rest on your laurels when you dominate the market, as British Leyland seemed to do in the 1970s, but one legacy of the often-troubled British Leyland years was a range of models that included more hits than misses. In the years before and after British Leyland, there have been some ground-breaking designs that have helped to shape the way the UK's buses have developed.

For years, bus design has been governed by the Construction and Use Regulations that dictated how long and wide buses and coaches for UK use should be, and these restricted how many seats could be provided for passengers. For many years, two-axle single-deckers could be 8.4m (27ft 6in) long and 2.3m (7ft 6in) wide, which meant a bus typically had seats for 35 passengers, sometimes up to 40 with clever design. Two-axle double-deckers could be the same width but only 7.9m (26ft) long, and 56-seaters were very much the norm. Three-axle buses, still a minority choice in the 1930s and 1940s, could be 9.1m (30ft) long.

However, with the post-war travel boom in the late 1940s, bus operators lobbied for longer vehicles with space for more passengers. There was a slight concession in 1946, when buses could be

Driver-only operation – pay-as-you-enter – became increasingly popular in the cost-conscious 1960s. Willowbrook, part of the Duple Group by this time, was using this 1959 Grimsby-Cleethorpes 9.1m (30ft)-long AEC Reliance two-door bus in this February 1961 advert to feature the passenger capacity – 'A seating capacity of 42 with standing room for 18 – *a total of 60 passengers!*'. Later, in 1961, 11m (36ft)-long single-deckers became legal, greatly increasing possible passenger capacity.

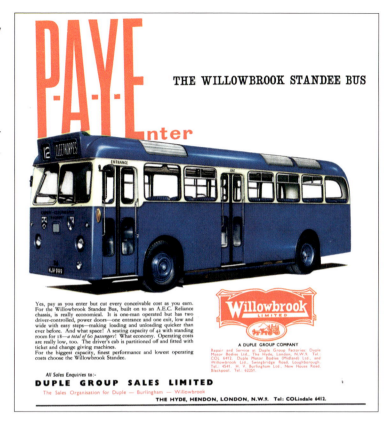

THE WILLOWBROOK STANDEE BUS

Yes, pay as you enter but cut every conceivable cost as you earn. For the Willowbrook Standee Bus, built on to an A.E.C. Reliance chassis, is really economical. It is one-man operated but has two driver-controlled, power doors—one entrance and one exit, low and wide with easy steps—making loading and unloading quicker than ever before. And what space! A seating capacity of 42 with standing room for 18—*a total of 60 passengers!* What economy. Operating costs are really low, too. The driver's cab is partitioned off and fitted with ticket and change giving machines.

For the biggest capacity, finest performance and lowest operating costs choose the Willowbrook Standee.

Willowbrook
LIMITED

A DUPLE GROUP COMPANY
Repair and Service at Duple Group Factories: Duple Motor Bodies Ltd., The Hyde, London, N.W.9. Tel: COL 6412. Duple Motor Bodies (Midland) Ltd., and Willowbrook Ltd., Swingbridge Road, Loughborough. Tel.: 4541. H. V. Burlingham Ltd., New House Road, Blackpool. Tel.: 62251.

All Sales Enquiries to:-
DUPLE GROUP SALES LIMITED
The Sales Organisation for Duple — Burlingham — Willowbrook

THE HYDE, HENDON, LONDON, N.W.9. Tel: COLindale 6412.

up to 2.4m (8ft) wide – if approved – and 9.1m (30ft) long; 2.4m (8ft) wide single-deckers became legal in 1950, while double-deckers could be 2.4m (8ft) wide but had to be content with a slight length increase to 8.2m (27ft). For the new breed of underfloor-engined single-deckers, that meant up to 45 seats could be provided; for double-deckers, 66 seated passengers could now be legally squeezed in. From 1956, double-deckers could be up to 9.1m (30ft) long, and there was a rush to buy front-engined models with up to 74 seats, sometimes with forward entrances rather than the rear entrances of the majority of their predecessors. The 9.1m (30ft) length paved the way for a totally new breed of double-decker, with a rear-mounted engine and seats for up to 78 passengers.

Further relaxation of the regulations from 1961 did not distinguish between single-deck and double-deck buses, so 11m (36ft) became the maximum permitted length and maximum width was relaxed to 2.5m (8ft 2½in). Then, 12m (39ft 4in) long by 2.5m (8ft 2½in) wide became the UK standard, allowing manufacturers and operators a great deal more scope.

In recent years, the maximum length for a two-axle bus has been stretched to 13.5m (44ft 3in) and the maximum width to 2.55m (8ft 4in), while three-axle buses can be up to 15m (49ft 2in) long. Articulated buses can be 18.75m (61ft 6in) long – more than twice as long as the relaxed 1950 regulations for rigid single-deck buses allowed.

There were also external influences on bus design when the UK government announced its New Bus Grants scheme in 1968. To boost bus sales and hasten the move towards driver-only operation, the government would meet 25 per cent of the cost of new buses that were suitable for driver-only operation. So the scheme spelt the end of the front-engined double-decker, still the bus of choice for some municipal fleets, and with the newly formed PTEs preparing to absorb some very mixed municipal fleets

FirstBus was an early customer for articulated single-deckers, regarded by some as an alternative to the double-decker. This 2005 First Greater Manchester Scania 58-seat N94UA artic is in Manchester in 2016.

over the next six years, there was an opportunity to invest heavily in new standardised buses, particularly when the Bus Grant went up to 50 per cent and stayed at that level throughout the 1970s, until it was gradually reduced and phased out by 1984. This was all good news for operators and meant that they were better placed to ride out the early post-deregulation years from the mid-1980s. The manufacturers, who saw the demand for full-size buses plummet after 1984, were less than happy.

Looking back, the period from the late 1920s to the late 1940s was generally one of evolution, with the interruption of World War Two, when minds were concentrated in other directions. However, from 1950 onwards, the bus builders bounced back with revolutionary ideas that reinvented the humble bus, and that revolution has continued since as buses became bigger, engine positions changed, and environmental concerns led to the trusty diesel engine becoming cleaner and more acceptable, and also to the spread of alternatives to the diesel – diesel-electric hybrids, battery electric, gas and even hydrogen fuel-cell buses.

Chapter 2
Who built the buses?

Back in the 1950s, when bus operators bought all their buses from UK manufacturers, there were suppliers and models to fit every perceived need. There were 16 chassis builders and 19 bodybuilders supplying the bulk of the market's needs, plus 'in-house' builders with a restricted group of customers.

The major builders were AEC, Daimler, Guy and Leyland – all well-established and with the capacity to supply chassis in quantity. Guy had come to prominence during the war as a builder of rugged and reliable buses. Daimler also built private cars, and the others also built trucks and other commercial vehicles.

Next were the lower-capacity builders – like Albion, Crossley and Dennis – who often relied on repeat orders from faithful customers, and some relative newcomers to the bus market – like Atkinson, Foden, Seddon, and Sentinel – who were tempted to dip a toe in the bus market at a time when the major builders were working to capacity, often with export orders, and UK bus operators were crying out for new buses to replace elderly vehicles that had stayed in service during World War Two, long past their normal withdrawal date.

Then there was Bedford, a major chassis builder that tended to concentrate on lightweight coaches and had never even nibbled at the big bus market. Plus, the two 'in-house' builders: BMMO (Birmingham

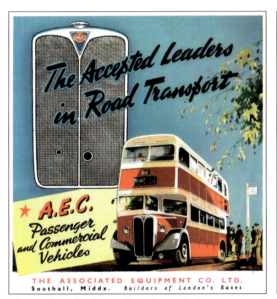

Above left: In the days before the Trades Descriptions Act, AEC boasted that they were 'The Accepted Leaders in Road Transport' in this 1948 trade press advert. Certainly, AEC and rival Leyland dominated sales to UK operators at the time.

Above right: Daimler also made boastful claims. Its COG5 model, featured in this 1936 advert, was a popular choice for municipal bus fleets, and was well regarded, though perhaps not 'The finest bus chassis in the world'.

Guy really established its reputation during World War Two, when its Arab chassis with Gardner engine became one of the types available for bus-hungry operators. Many bus companies that had been allocated Guy Arabs during the war went on to choose the model in the post-war period. This is a preserved 1946 London Transport example with no-frills Park Royal 56-seat body.

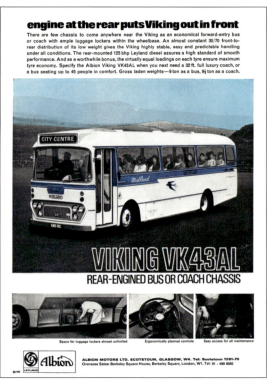

Above left: Although Leyland enjoyed a much smaller proportion of London Transport orders than AEC, it used an illustration of one of its Titan RTL types in this 1962 advert, proclaiming that '73% of all British bus operating municipalities' used its buses. Other contemporary Leyland types are also featured.

Above right: Glasgow-based Albion was one of Leyland's first acquisitions, in 1951, and it continued to produce its own model range, often for Scottish and export markets. The rear-engined Viking VK43L was popular with SBG companies looking for a lighter-weight chassis to replace older front-engined types. All SBG's Vikings had Alexander Y type bodies, like the Alexander (Midland) 1965 example in this 1967 advert.

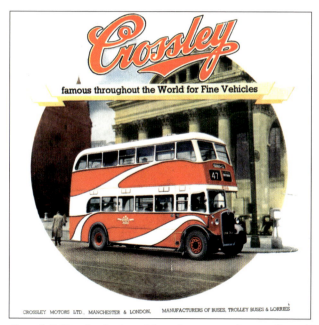

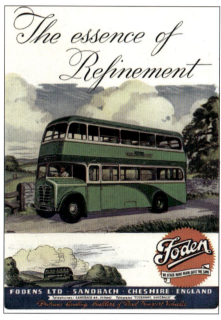

Above left: Manchester-based Crossley was a major supplier to Manchester Corporation. This 1938 Crossley Mancunian with distinctive Manchester Corporation/Crossley 54-seat body was featured in this 1939 advert.

Above right: Truck builder Foden ventured into bus chassis building in the 1930s and used this illustration of a mythical PVD6 with a forward entrance body in this 1947 advert. It would be another decade before there was a wide acceptance of forward entrances on double-deckers, but Foden's distinctive full-width front was the first of many to appear on chassis available on the open market.

and Midland Motor Omnibus), building only for Midland Red, and state-owned Bristol and ECW, which could only build for the other state-owned fleets – Tilling, Scottish Bus and London Transport. As builders for specific operators, BMMO and Bristol/ECW pioneered some important types, like underfloor-engined single-deckers and low-height double-deckers.

Bodywork for the open market was provided by 18 builders. Some like Burlingham, Duple and Plaxton concentrated on the coach market, sometimes building bus bodies in the summer months; others were low-volume builders – Beadle, Mann Egerton, Massey, Reading, Saunders-Roe, Strachans. The big-order builders were Alexander, Crossley, Leyland, Metro-Cammell-Weymann, Northern Counties, Park Royal, Roe and Willowbrook.

The trend-setting Bristol/ECW Lodekka was only available to state-owned bus fleets, so there was no need to advertise its products, although an early Wilts & Dorset Lodekka did feature in this 1957 British Aluminium trade advert.

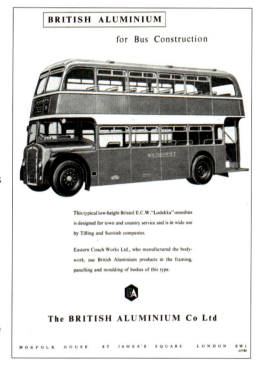

Bristol and ECW products became widely available after the Leyland–Bristol share exchange in 1965. London Transport, which did buy some ECW bodies while it was in state ownership, bought Bristol LH6Ls with 39-seat ECW bodies in 1976.

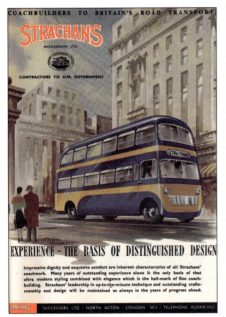

Above left: Strachans Successors never achieved spectacular sales in the post-war period but produced this impressive, but imagined, illustration of a full-fronted double-decker in 1947, as a foretaste of a possible future.

Above right: MCW, the sales organisation for Metro-Cammell and Weymann bodies, was a major force on the UK bus bodybuilding scene. This illustration from 1961 features buses in imaginary liveries – a Leyland Atlantean, an AEC Reliance BET-style bus, a forward entrance double-decker and a Weymann-bodied AEC Reliance coach.

By the mid-1950s, the situation was already changing following a period of acquisition activity. AEC had bought Crossley, Maudslay, Park Royal and Roe, now together in the ACV (Associated Commercial Vehicles) Group, and Leyland had bought Albion. This was merely the start of a process that would leave only Alexander, Dennis and Plaxton still manufacturing in 2022 from that 1954 list of 39 builders.

However, just as names have disappeared, new UK-based names have sprung up, and now even buses built in mainland Europe and as far away as China – unthinkable in 1954 – are running on UK roads.

Just how the bus manufacturing industry got from the 1954 tally to today's international situation is worth recording, as it shows how operators react to near-monopolies and encourage newcomers to provide alternatives – and shows how near-monopolies tried to dictate what operators buy and, arguably, stifled innovation.

By 1961, both Daimler and Guy were part of the Jaguar group, while Leyland was mopping up car and truck builders. In 1962 came the biggest Leyland *coup* to date – its merger (really a take-over) of its deadliest rival, AEC, which came with chassis builders Crossley and Maudslay and bodybuilders Park Royal and Roe. Leyland then created the Leyland Motor Corporation that, in 1965, acquired 25 per cent of the shares in state-owned Bristol and ECW, which brought these products back on to the open market after more than 15 years.

Jaguar, meanwhile, had merged with the British Motor Corporation to form British Motor Holdings (BMH), while on the car side, Leyland added Rover to Standard-Triumph. All of these players came together in 1968, when Leyland and BMH combined as British Leyland, which meant that, on the bus side, AEC, Bristol, Crossley, Daimler, ECW, Guy, Maudslay, Park Royal and Roe were now under common ownership, resulting in duplication of models that led to the inevitable thinning-out process. British Leyland made it clear that many popular models would be dropped from the lists to be replaced by new models that were expected to have universal appeal.

First to go were rear-engined single-deck types to clear the way for the new Leyland National city bus, a complete highly standardised integrally constructed bus. This joint Leyland–National Bus Company initiative saw off the popular Bristol RE, as well as the AEC Swift and Leyland Panther ranges, and the unloved Daimler Roadliner.

The Leyland National was a brave venture involving Leyland and the National Bus Company. Although it never achieved its sales potential, it enjoyed success in the absence of much competition. National Bus fleets were, inevitably, major customers, and this 1976 East Kent 11.3m (37ft)-long 49-seat example is seen at Dover in 1978.

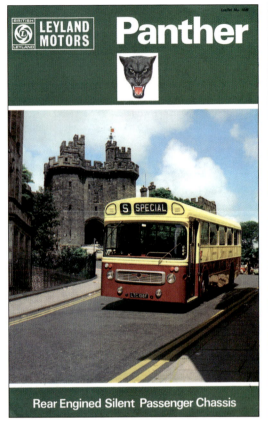

Above left: Leyland's Panther was one of the new breed of rear-engined single-deck chassis introduced in the early 1960s, but was swept away by the arrival of the Leyland National in the 1970s. This 1968 brochure features a new Lancaster Corporation Panther with 53-seat East Lancs body; buses like this came close to matching the seating capacity of the older double-deckers they often replaced.

Above right: After it became available to all operators, the Bristol RE was widely recognised as the best of the first tranche of rear-engined single-deck chassis. This 1966 Bristol advert features an impression of a two-door ECW-bodied RELL example.

Not all bus companies were happy about what was turning into a virtual monopoly for British Leyland and wanted to regain some influence in the models they chose. Then, truck-builder Seddon produced the RU, a Bristol RE equivalent with the ever-popular Gardner engine, and later what was conceived as a Gardner-engined Leyland Leopard, the Pennine 7.

Metro-Cammell-Weymann's (MCW) initial response to Leyland's market domination was to team up with Scania to develop the single-deck Metro-Scania and double-deck Metropolitan. The other Swedish giant, Volvo, tested the market with its rear-engined B59 urban single-deck model, but achieved great success with its B58 and B10M underfloor-engined chassis. Leyland had arguably opened the doors to the importers who often had to weigh the expense of converting their chassis to right-hand drive against the likelihood of UK orders. Bus and coach builders from France, Germany, Italy, Netherlands and Scandinavia – indeed much of mainland Europe – tested the UK market with varying degrees of success.

There was a new UK name, Optare, which rose from the ashes of Roe's Leeds coachbuilding plant in 1985 and quickly established a reputation for stylish coachwork, first on other chassis and then increasingly turning to the production of complete vehicles. Subsequently, ownership of Optare

Right: Manufacturers recognised that Leyland's near-monopoly restricted the choice of available models, and MCW combined with Scania to market the Metro-Scania for the UK market, based on an existing Scania model. This is the cover for a 1969 leaflet promoting this Swedish-British alliance.

Below: Volvo saw opportunities in the UK bus and coach market with two underfloor-engined models – the B58 and its successor, the B10M. Stagecoach became an enthusiastic customer for the B10M, as seen here with Alexander PS type 49-seat body, a 1993 delivery to Stagecoach Scotland in the Stagecoach Group's hometown of Perth.

Volvo later introduced a series of successful rear-engined single-deck chassis and, while most carried bodies built in the UK, some were built further afield. This 2003 B7L with Spanish-built Hispano 41-seat body, first registered by Volvo at Warwick, is here in service in 2012 with the fast-growing Scottish independent fleet of McGill's.

Left: The Irisbus Agora, a Renault-designed bus built in France but completed in the UK by Optare, failed to make much impression on the UK market. This 2003 Agoraline is one of 14 bought by Norfolk County Council for Park & Ride services in Norwich.

Below: The neat low-floor Optare Solo was introduced in 1997 and went on to be produced in a range of sizes from 7.1m to 10.2m (23ft 3in to 33ft 5in) long, and in two different widths. This 2001 First Mainline 26-seat example, in Sheffield when new, is an 8.5m (27ft 9in)-long bus.

has changed on a surprisingly frequent basis; at various times, it was owned by United Bus, North American Bus Industries, Darwen Group and Ashok Leyland and, with a name change to Switch Mobility in 2020, it announced that it would no longer build diesel buses.

Then in 1987, Leyland Bus was bought by its management and just a year later sold out to Volvo Bus. A couple of Leyland models were allowed to stay on the lists, notably the Olympian, which enjoyed a few more years as a Volvo model. Meanwhile, MCW, another of the bus building giants, was sold by its new owners, leading to its closure.

Waiting in the wings, however, was one of Britain's longest-established bus builders. In recent years, Dennis had not built buses in any great volume until it introduced the double-deck Dominator chassis in 1977, plugging a gap for a Gardner-engined bus after Leyland discontinued its Fleetline. This was a successful move and led Dennis to widen its bus and coach chassis range. However, Dennis really came into its own with its Dart model in 1988 and, in particular, in 1995, when its Dart SLF brought an affordable low-floor single-decker on to the market.

Ownership of Dennis changed in the 1980s, and it found itself, along with the coachbuilders Alexander and Plaxton, struggling for its life when the Mayflower Group went into administration in 2004. This led to a management buyout at Plaxton, and Alexander and Dennis combining to create Alexander Dennis Ltd (ADL); in 2007, ADL bought Plaxton, and, in 2019, ADL was sold to the North American NFI Group.

The final piece of the jigsaw had been the expansion of Wrights of Ballymena, a well-established builder in Northern Ireland, into the mainstream UK market, where it achieved wide success with a series of attractive and innovative products. Wrights too had its problems and was reconstituted with new owners in 2019.

Although Dennis had been a relatively minor player in the bus market for many years, the Dominator double-deck chassis moved it into the big time, proving popular with operators looking for a Gardner rear-engined model to succeed Daimler's Fleetline. There is no mistaking who built the chassis on the front of this 1979 Hyndburn East Lancs-bodied 78-seater.

Wrights' StreetLite was introduced as an alternative lightweight, but greatly adaptable, low-floor integral single-deck model. Available in DF (door forward) or WF (wheel forward) versions, this is a 2013 First Hampshire & Dorset 37-seat 9m (29ft 6in)-long DF bus in Portsmouth in 2014.

Once, the great majority of buses bought for service in the UK combined a chassis from one builder with a body from another UK builder; the concept of buying a complete vehicle from one supplier was largely resisted, as it seemed to restrict the customer's ability to specify buses for its own particular requirements. On the other hand, some manufacturers recognised the commercial advantages of one-stop shopping and argued, with some justification, that this helped to guarantee quality and on-time delivery.

The situation changed over the years, with best-selling integral models like the Leyland National and the MCW Metrobus in the 1970s and 1980s, and since that time there has been a move by manufacturers to offer complete vehicles. Optare adopted this approach from the start, and although Alexander Dennis majors on complete vehicles, it will also body on other chassis. Volvo markets complete single-deck buses and coaches and works with selected bodybuilders for its main double-deck range. Wrights has moved from being purely a bodybuilder to producing complete vehicles.

While at one time these builders were principally supplying the UK market with diesel-engined buses, environmental concerns hastened a move to diesel-electric hybrid buses, gas buses, and increasingly to zero-emission battery-electric buses, and there is a growing interest in hydrogen fuel-cell buses. This has encouraged the existing suppliers to develop new models to suit this changing scenario and has seen the arrival of new entrants, particularly those offering electric vehicles; names like Arrival, BYD, Caetano and Equipmake are appearing on the UK bus scene, while established UK builders are introducing a wide range of electric single-deckers.

Chapter 3

Front-engined and underfloor-engined double-deckers

From the earliest days of the motor bus, the great majority of double-deckers had their engines firmly at the front and, for more than 60 years, the double-deck bus evolved. From solid-tyred, high-built open-toppers in the 1900s, where the driver sat behind the engine, to the forward control pneumatic-tyred models of the 1920s, there is a clear line of development. One bus that broke the mould was Leyland's low-built covered-top Titan TD1 of 1927, which set the standard for buses built over the next 40 years. Gradually, technical improvements, like diesel engines and preselector gearboxes, were incorporated in the specifications, often following the example of the RT type developed by AEC and London Transport in the late 1930s, which set a standard for post-war double-deckers, with its more powerful engine, preselect gearbox and smooth body shape. Bodybuilders developed attractive styles and, when vehicle weights were under scrutiny, worked to introduce lighter-weight bodies.

Arguably the father of all front-engined models that followed it over the next 40 years, the Leyland Titan TD1 reimagined the UK double-deck bus as a practical low-built bus. This is a preserved 1928 TD1 with lowbridge Leyland 51-seat body in Glasgow in 1994.

When longer double-deckers were permitted from 1956, operators welcomed the ability to squeeze up to eight extra seats into a 9.1m (30ft) double-decker. Others specified a forward entrance behind the front axle, in place of the more familiar rear platform usually open but sometimes with doors.

The bus companies were watching the impact that Leyland's new rear-engined Atlantean was having on the double-deck market. Traditional front-engined double-deckers continued in production and in popularity, however, with some operators to the end of the 1960s. London Transport decided to replace its trolleybuses in the 1950s and 1960s with what was, at first glance, an old-fashioned double-decker – the Routemaster. However, the Routemaster was never an anachronism; its open rear platform was well suited to London conditions, technically it boasted an advanced specification, and many Routemasters outlasted successive double-deck and single-deck rear-engined 'off the peg' models.

Another operator designing buses for its own use was Midland Red, whose ultimate front-engined double-decker was the BMMO D9, introduced in 1958 – an integrally constructed vehicle with independent front suspension, of which 344 were built.

Although the popular Leyland rear-engined Atlantean was already on the market in 1959, the newly arrived legendary London Transport Routemaster, built by AEC and Park Royal, was technically very advanced, and the open rear entrance was regarded as essential for London service. The longer RML type here is a 72-seater, working for Arriva following the privatisation of London's buses. The Routemaster family had long lives – this 1965 example was still in front-line service when photographed in Oxford Street in 2003, demonstrating the hop-on/hop-off facility popular with Londoners.

The lives of some of London's Routemasters were prolonged thanks to refurbishment by Marshall. Fresh from its refurb, and painted in all-over red, this 1962 Routemaster is at Golders Green in 2001.

Like the Routemaster, the BMMO D9, developed solely for Midland Red use, was a later model that was bristling with advanced features, such as integral construction and disc brakes. This preserved 1966 D9 with Willowbrook 72-seat body is at Toddington in 2017. (Sholto Thomas)

Two double-deck models bucked the trend and featured entrances ahead of the front wheels, with the front platform sharing the space with the engine and the driver. First was the Guy Wulfrunian in 1959, built primarily for the independent West Riding company, with a bulky Gardner 6LX engine on the front overhang. Like the Routemaster, the Wulfrunian bristled with new features, in this case air suspension, disc brakes and independent front suspension, but it attracted barely any sales outside the sponsoring West Riding company. Of the 137 built, all but 10 went to West Riding.

A similar approach was adopted for the Ailsa, which started life as a concept by Volvo importer Ailsa Trucks, with encouragement from the conservative SBG. It used a much more compact front-mounted engine than the Wulfrunian and a simpler specification and went on to achieve some success in the UK and in export markets.

Much earlier, the success of underfloor-engined single-deckers prompted some manufacturers to consider this layout for double-deckers. They appeared at times when there was less concern about high

Guy's 1959 Wulfrunian was developed, as stated in this 1960 trade advert, to 'An operator's specification'; the operator was the independent West Riding company, which bought all but a few of the 137 produced. What distinguished the Wulfrunian from other contemporary models was the front-mounted engine, a hefty Gardner 6LX, which shared the front platform with the cramped driver's cab and the passenger entrance. In spite of an advanced specification, it was not the success hoped for. The bus in the advert is West Riding's 1959 prototype, with 75-seat Roe body.

Above: The Ailsa marked a return to a front-engined layout when it was launched in 1973, but it used a more compact Volvo engine and went on to relative success after it was officially adopted by Volvo. London Buses tried three Ailsas in comparative trials with Dennis, Leyland and MCW double-deck models. This bus, new in 1984, differed from the others with both front and rear entrances, seen here in Wandsworth in 1985. (Tony Wilson)

Left: Derby City Transport sampled various double-deck models in the 1980s, including the Dennis Dominator, Leyland Olympian and MCW Metrobus. This is a 1982 Volvo Ailsa with 73-seat Northern Counties body in 1985.

floorlines, and another consequence of the engine position was its effect on overall height restrictions. First was the AEC Regent IV, developed from its Regal IV single-deck range, but destined never to get beyond the experimental stage. Then, Midland Red, which had successfully pioneered the use of underfloor-engined single-deckers with its own-build BMMO S6 types, decided to build two underfloor-engined D10 double-deckers in 1961, and while these were used successfully, no more examples were built.

More than 20 years later, Volvo developed the underfloor-engined Citybus, a model based on the chassis of its highly successful B10M model. This proved successful in UK and spurred Leyland into action to develop the Lion, based on a single-deck model built by its Danish subsidiary, DAB. In its short life on the model lists, just 32 were built, and it was no surprise when Volvo acquired Leyland Bus that the Lion was quietly dropped.

Lacking a rear-engined double-deck model, Volvo also tested the waters with a double-deck version of the successful B10M horizontal mid-engined single-deck chassis. This is the prototype, built for Strathclyde PTE with an 86-seat Marshall body. The model achieved some success as the Volvo Citybus.

Right: The London General fleet of London Buses bought the Volvo B10M Citybus with 80-seat Northern Counties body in 1989. The horizontal mid-mounted engine made for a high floorline, evident from the lower deck window line, at a time when bus manufacturers and operators were starting to look for easier access for passengers.

Below: Leyland's response to the underfloor-engined Volvo double-deckers was the Lion, based on a single-deck chassis produced by DAB, Leyland's Danish subsidiary. Few were built – this is a 1989 delivery to Eastern Scottish with 86-seat Alexander body in 1990.

Chapter 4

Low-height double-deckers

The word 'low' was not really in the vocabulary of early bus designers. They seemed to accept that the height of the frame on early 20th century double-deckers would inevitably affect the overall height of the bodied bus. These were essentially urban buses, and if there were low railway or other bridges, then they could avoid them or use single-deckers.

Then, as the number of buses increased and travel by bus became more popular, operators wanted to use double-deckers on interurban and even rural routes. By the mid-1920s, closed-top double-deckers were becoming the norm, and they were becoming much lower built. In 1927, Leyland's new Titan model had introduced the novel concept of a sunken offside upper deck gangway that led to awkward high-mounted four-across seats. This 'lowbridge' arrangement (just 3.96m [13ft] high) was not an ideal layout, but it allowed operators to run double-deckers rather than single-deckers on many routes. This model was also available in 'Hybridge' layout (4.27m [14ft] height), with normal seating on both decks. Although it was awkward, the lowbridge layout was still being specified by a few operators into the early 1960s.

The pioneering low-height Bristol/ECW Lodekka was in production for state-owned fleets between 1953 and 1968. The original LD series was succeeded by the flat-floor F series; this is a 1965 60-seat FS6B in service with York-West Yorkshire in 1979. The Lodekka offered proper seating on the upper deck in preference to the awkward lowbridge layout on earlier Bristol/ECW models; lowbridge-bodied double-deckers on other chassis continued in production into the 1960s.

Above left: Noting the success of the Lodekka, AEC introduced the lowheight Bridgemaster model, followed by the Renown, as featured here in this 1965 advert showing an East Yorkshire Park Royal 70-seat Renown demonstrating its flexibility by passing through the ancient Beverley Bar.

Above right: Dennis negotiated to build the Lodekka under licence as the Loline. This 1958 trade advert, produced before Loline production had started, used an image of a typical Tilling Bristol/ECW Lodekka, doctored to show the Loline frontal design.

Below: Leyland responded to calls for a low-height chassis with the Lowlander, built by Albion in Glasgow and badged as an Albion for Scottish customers. SBG companies bought Lowlanders – these three 1963 examples in Grangemouth depot of Alexander (Midland) in 1979 carry Alexander 71-seat bodies with two different destination layouts in evidence.

Bristol and ECW solved the lowbridge problem with the low-height Lodekka model in 1949 – a low-built double-decker (4.09m [13ft 5in] high) with normal seating on both decks. Bristol/ECW products were only available to state-owned fleets at the time, and so others tried to replicate the layout for the open market – AEC with its Bridgemaster and Renown models, Dennis with the Loline and Leyland-Albion with the Lowlander; the Loline was essentially the Lodekka built under licence. All achieved only limited success – the Loline was most popular with just 280 sales, but none came anywhere near the 5,000-plus Lodekkas that were built. The Lodekka proved to be a reliable and long-lived model, which was attractive to passengers thanks to its combination of a low entrance and normal upper deck seating.

By the late 1990s, it was probably inevitable that, following lowbridge and low-height types, low-floor double-deckers would follow quickly after the success of easy access single-deckers.

SBG companies were so happy with the Bristol/ECW Lodekka that they exchanged troublesome newer rear-engined Bristol VRTs for Lodekkas from National Bus Company fleets. This FLF6G Lodekka with ECW 70-seat forward entrance body in Edinburgh in 1978 was new to Brighton Hove & District in 1967.

Chapter 5

Underfloor-engined single-deckers

By the end of the 1930s, the typical British single-deck bus had a front-mounted diesel engine to the left of the driver and a saloon behind with around 35 seats; its entrance was just behind the front axle or just behind the rear axle. Some bus companies looked to cram more passengers into the maximum permitted 8.4m (27ft 6in) length, and the way to do this was to reduce the space taken up by the engine and driver so that another row of seats could be squeezed in. To highlight two examples: this gave the Northern General company 38-seaters and the SMT Group 39-seaters. A few operators in the 1920s and 1930s took advantage of the regulation that permitted single-deck buses with three axles to be 9.1m (30ft) long, enabling more seats to be fitted, but three-axle models were few and far between.

Manufacturers were conscious of the operators' desire for more seats and were working on innovative ways that could achieve this. AEC developed its Q model for the London General company in 1932, with its engine mounted behind the driver on the offside. Working with London Transport, Leyland built the underfloor-engined TF in 1937 and the little rear-engined CR type in 1938, and AEC had built an underfloor-engined prototype for Canada, just before the outbreak of World War Two called time out on anything but the most essential work.

An early attempt to reposition the engine was the AEC Q, first introduced in 1932. On the Q, the engine was longitudinally on the offside, behind the driver. London Transport was the main customer for the Q for both its Central and Country Area routes, taking 238 between 1932 and 1937, including five double-deckers – one a three-axle bus. This preserved 1935 Q with Birmingham Railway Carriage & Wagon company 37-seat body has a sliding door behind the front axle. Other London Qs had an entrance ahead of the front axle, anticipating the layout that would become popular from the 1950s.

We are privileged to announce
an order for

87

LEYLAND

FLAT-ENGINED COACHES

from

LONDON TRANSPORT

PRIVATE

LEYLAND MOTORS LTD · LEYLAND · LANCS

The Leyland TF, described in this 1938 advert as a flat-engined coach, had a horizontal engine. This is the 1937 prototype with Leyland-built 34-seat body. The other 87 TFs had a neater front-end arrangement.

It was not that underfloor or rear-mounted engines were particularly new. Büssing in Germany had developed an underfloor-engined bus in the 1930s, and most North American transit buses had rear-mounted engines by the late 1930s. While normal upright engines could be mounted at the rear, the mid-engined layout required a flat 'pancake' engine mounted under the floor, and that released the maximum interior space for passengers.

After the war, as UK manufacturers moved back from essential war work to supplying bus-hungry operators, most met this demand by offering chassis that were essentially updated versions of their pre-war range. There was also pressure to export as many buses as possible to help rebuild the UK economy, so innovation was not necessarily at the top of the agenda.

The first moves that challenged the accepted design of single-deckers came not from the major builders but from a major bus operator and a low-volume bus manufacturer. Midland Red, the 1,800-bus giant covering the West Midlands and well beyond, had been building buses mainly for its own fleet since 1924. In the pre-war period, it had built four experimental rear-engined single-deckers but during the war decided to convert them to an underfloor-engined layout. Later in the war years, a fifth prototype was built, a chassis-less bus with a mid-mounted underfloor engine, and the success of these buses led Midland Red to break the mould and go into production with 100 of its 40-seat S6 model in 1946, the first large fleet of underfloor-engined buses in the UK.

Next up was Shrewsbury-based Sentinel, famous for its steam lorries, and certainly not a big name in the bus business. It introduced its underfloor-engined STC4 model in 1948, which sold mainly to independent operators, but achieved something of a *coup* with an order from the Leyland-dominated Ribble fleet in 1949. As the Leyland plant was firmly in Ribble territory, this was doubtless a wake-up call to Leyland Motors, and, from 1951, Leyland's underfloor-engined models started to join the fleet in substantial numbers.

Leyland's first underfloor model was, in fact, a complete integral bus: the Olympic, developed with bodybuilders MCW and introduced in 1949. Integral buses do not require a chassis, as the bodywork is built directly on to the running units, which results in a sturdy and lighter-weight bus but denies operators the opportunity to specify their own bodywork from their favoured builders. To meet this demand, Leyland developed the Royal Tiger chassis, but regularly revisited the concept of integral models over the next 20 years. Export customers tended to be more enthusiastic about integrals, and successive models of the Olympic remained on Leyland's lists until 1971.

The BMMO S6, built in-house for Midland Red, was the first horizontal underfloor-engined model to go into production that anticipated the shape and layout of thousands more that would be built by a range of manufacturers from the 1950s onwards. While the major builders were struggling to pick up where they left off before World War Two, as well as meeting export commitments, Midland Red had 100 40-seat S6s in service in 1946, with bodies by Brush and, in this case, Metro-Cammell.

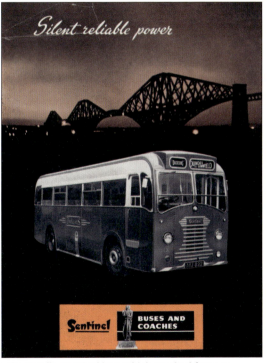

Above left: Although it never achieved great sales success, the Beadle-Sentinel bus, which resulted from co-operation between Beadle of Chatham and Sentinel of Shrewsbury, was a clear indication of the future shape and layout of buses when it first appeared in 1948.

Above right: Sentinel was quick with a commercially available underfloor-engined single-deck model, the STC4. The bus in this 1950 advert features a newly delivered 40-seat bus for Dickson of Dundee.

When Leyland caught up with an underfloor-engined model, it was a chassis-less integral bus, the Olympic, built in conjunction with MCW. This 1950 advert features one of the 40-seat prototypes.

AEC, too, recognised the advantages of integral models, but accepted that many customers were simply looking for a chassis that could be bodied to suit their operation. So, the Regal IV, introduced in 1949, fulfilled that role. As did other builders' first-generation mid-engined heavyweight models like the Daimler Freeline and Guy Arab UF, as well as models from less mainstream builders like Atkinson and Dennis. These tended to be big-engined chassis, often with horizontal versions of the engines that powered contemporary double-deckers, and they were necessary as many of the early underfloor-engined single-deckers weighed as much as their double-deck counterparts. This was at a time when bus operators were becoming so concerned about the cost of fuelling these heavy buses that they started insisting on lighter buses. The substantial chassis and engines of buses of the early 1950s contributed greatly to the unladen weight, so the pressure was on both the chassis and body manufacturers to come up with considerably lighter buses.

The manufacturers responded quickly for the demand for lighter chassis, so the AEC Reliance, Guy Arab LUF and Leyland Tiger Cub became the main choices for the UK market, often with less powerful engines but greatly reduced unladen weights.

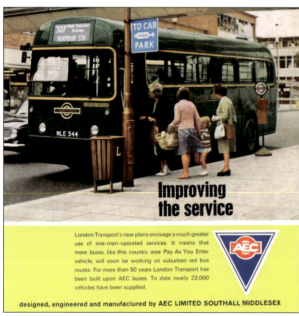

AEC's response to the demand for underfloor-engined chassis was the Regal IV, a heavyweight model like most of the early models. London Transport was the major home market customer for the Regal IV, and, in the absence of anything newer, AEC used this 1953 Metro-Cammell-bodied bus built for LT's Country Area services in an advert that appeared 11 years later, anticipating orders for the new breed of driver-only buses.

Bristol, by that time building only for the state-owned Tilling, Scottish Bus and London Transport fleets, developed the integral LS (Light Saloon) and later the chassis-and-body MW (Medium Weight) with its partner ECW, while AEC kept its options open with the integral Monocoach with Park Royal and Alexander bodywork. The LS and MW were very successful in their captive market; on the open market, the great majority of AEC customers preferred the Reliance chassis to the integral Monocoach.

Right: Concerns from bus operators about the unladen weight and consequent effect on fuel consumption led to demands for lighter-weight chassis; the heavier chassis often weighed as much as contemporary double-deck buses that had at least 10 more seats. Leyland's answer was the Tiger Cub, and the 1952 advert makes great play that a full-size bus had a kerbside weight of less than six tons. The bus featured is a Leyland demonstrator with distinctive Saro 44-seat body.

Below: Bristol and ECW replaced their integral LS model with the MW (Medium Weight) chassis, and this became the standard single-deck bus for Tilling companies. This 1965 MW6G model with 45-seat ECW body is at Newport later in its life, following the creation of the National Bus Company. (Sholto Thomas)

By 1950, single-deck buses could be up to 9.1m (30ft) long, and with no engine intrusion in the saloon, underfloor-engined models could offer seats for up to 45 passengers. Not surprisingly, orders for new heavyweight front-engined single-deckers quickly plummeted. In 1961, the legislation was relaxed to permit 11m (36ft)-long buses, so 53-seat single-deckers became the norm in many places. These offered almost as many seats as older double-deckers, resulting in many fleets replacing time-served double-deckers with these types.

The move to longer buses essentially ended the ultra-lightweight era, and there was a move to more powerful engines to suit the larger buses. The Reliance, which had started as a lighter-weight model, continued as AEC's main mid-engined offering, and Leyland created the Leopard. Both models would remain on the lists until 1979 (Reliance) and 1982 (Leopard), mainly for coach customers, but also for conservative customers like SBG, which was not convinced about models like Leyland's National and wanted sturdy, proven chassis carrying bodies from its favoured builders. When Leyland proved unwilling to offer its Leopard with a Gardner engine, SBG turned to Seddon to build the Pennine 7, essentially a Gardner-powered Leopard, but, as we shall see, there were other developments that would influence the configuration of single-deck buses in the 1960s and 1970s.

The larger-engined Leyland Leopard became popular when 11m (36ft)-long buses were legalised in 1961, and independent operators like Graham's of Paisley bought new and second-hand Leopards. These Leopards carry bodies by (from left) Duple, Alexander and Plaxton; the Duple-bodied bus was new to Graham's in 1978, the Alexander bus started life in 1970 as an experimental Leyland chassis, and the Plaxton was new in 1969 to a South Yorkshire operator.

AEC's popular Reliance grew into a heavier-weight bigger-engined model when 11m (36ft) buses arrived. This 1971 model with 49-seat BET-style Marshall body was new to City of Oxford in 1971 and, ten years later, had passed to the Oxfordshire independent operator Chiltern Queens.

Above: The Gardner-engined Seddon Pennine 7 was popular with some SBG companies, for whom it was designed. This is the 1973 prototype with Alexander 49-seat body for Eastern Scottish when new.

Right: The Dennis Dorchester was another model aimed at operators that wanted a Gardner engine, but few were built. Central Scottish operated this 1984 example with Alexander TE 49-seat dual-purpose bodywork.

There was still a demand for mid-engined chassis into the 1990s after Volvo had successfully broken into the UK market with the B58 and later B10M models, and Leyland responded with the Tiger – which, bowing to pressure, was also offered with a Gardner engine. Although there was some reluctance on Volvo's part to abandon the mid-engined layout, particularly for coaching work, its competitors were moving decisively to rear-engined types, and eventually Volvo did the same.

Two manufacturers that had stuck with front-engined chassis, catering mainly for the coach market, were Bedford and Ford. In 1970, Bedford introduced the first of its mid-engined Y-series chassis, unusually with a vertical rather than horizontal engine. Ford stuck with front-mounted engines to the left of the driver, but, from 1977, the engine was underfloor-mounted – though still at the front. Several larger fleets bought examples for bus work, mainly attracted by the prospect of a less expensive and lighter full-size bus.

An inevitable consequence of an engine mounted under the floor was a high floor line, and, while this was less of a problem for coaches, bus operators were becoming more aware of the difficulties that people with disabilities had when boarding a high-floor bus and the increasing demand for easily accessible buses.

Left: Volvo's B10M sold well to UK operators in coach and bus form. Burnley & Pendle bought this Alexander P type 53-seater in 1988. The severe lines of the P type body are improved by the attractive livery.

Below: Bedford's Y-series, its first underfloor-engined chassis, appeared in 1970, and the 11m (36ft)-long YRT was a popular model. It is here with a Plaxton Derwent 55-seat body bought in 1974 by York Pullman.

Chapter 6

Small buses

T he bus operators that have had the greatest influence on bus design have tended to be the big fleets; over the years, these were the big groups, the major municipal and later PTE fleets, and the larger independents – and, in broad terms, they had been looking for buses that provided maximum passenger capacity for the lowest operating cost. Manufacturers responded by offering buses that were often lighter, to ensure better fuel consumption figures, but still provided seating capacity to maintain fares revenue.

Independent operators, often with rural and semi-rural services, survived on cast-offs from the larger fleets and occasionally splashed out on new buses. The little 29-seat Bedford OB, most often bought for coaching duties, was often found on bus duties in the 1950s, where its compact size, passenger capacity and low operating costs ensured that many marginal bus services survived.

However, when these buses had reached the end of the road, where could these operators turn? And it was not just the small independents that faced this issue. Many of the big company fleets had marginal services that were often operated by full-size buses in the absence of something more suitable.

It was Albion, part of the growing Leyland empire since 1951, that came up with an answer in 1955. The Nimbus was essentially a scaled-down (7.24m [23ft 9in] long) version of the underfloor-engined single-deck chassis the 'big boys' were buying. Uniquely, perhaps, it was based on a goods vehicle, Albion's unusual underfloor-engined Claymore model, and although it did not set the heather on fire, it proved to be a useful short-gap solution.

The Albion Nimbus, introduced in 1956, was an attempt to provide what was in effect a scaled-down underfloor-engined single-decker. The result was a neat little bus, as the 1958 Devon General Willowbrook-bodied bus featured shows, but it may have been ahead of its time and sales were disappointing.

MORE POWER TO A LIGHTWEIGHT'S PUNCH

The NEW Albion Nimbus

with increased engine power costs less to buy and less to run

Once again Albion achieve the near impossible. They've built an entirely new Nimbus chassis . . . they've packed it with advance-design features . . . yet at the same time they've *cut the price*.

And that's not the only saving. With engine power stepped up to 70 b.h.p., new easy change 4-speed gearbox and high capacity spiral bevel rear axle, running costs and maintenance charges are kept at rock-bottom level.

Ideal for feeder services or routes of low traffic density, this 31-seater's fully laden weight is under 6 tons while its overall length of 23' 3" and turning circle of 47 ft. ensure maximum manoeuvrability.

There's going to be a rush for the Nimbus when the news gets around . . . don't have any regrets later, place your order now and make 1959 your record low-cost operating year.

※ 70 b.h.p. underfloor engine giving high fuel economy

※ Gross laden weight with 31 passengers under 6 tons

※ One man operation

※ Low initial cost

ALBION MOTORS LTD.
SCOTSTOUN, GLASGOW, W.4.
Sales Division: HANOVER HOUSE, HANOVER SQUARE, LONDON, W.I.   Tel: MAYfair 8561

Bristol's solution to less economic routes was the SC, a lightweight front-engined integral bus bodied by ECW and available to state-owned fleets, though only Tilling companies bought any. It was succeeded by the SU model with an Albion underfloor engine – in many ways the Nimbus reborn.

For fleets that were unable to buy Bristol and ECW products in the 1950s and early 1960s, the choice was more limited. Dennis built a normal control version of its Falcon for faithful customers Aldershot & District, and Guy produced a special chassis based on its Vixen model, which with 26-seat ECW bodywork formed London's 84-strong GS class for less demanding Country Area work.

Left: The Tilling Group companies identified a need for smaller buses, often for more rural routes, and Bristol and ECW first developed the SC model and then the SU. This 1965 36-seat Western National SUL4A example is in Minehead in 1977. Like the Nimbus, the SU used an Albion engine. (Tony Wilson)

Below: When London Transport needed small buses for its Country Area, it turned to Guy for a version of its Vixen model and to ECW for the neat 26-seat bodywork. This 1953 GS type is one of more than 20 of the 84 built that survive in preservation.

When most of the major customers – the municipal and company-owned operators – were still buying ever-larger buses with the maximum number of seats, the major builders rarely produced models for the low-volume small bus market. And when they did, like Leyland's Albion Nimbus, the take-up was limited.

The spotlight was firmly on small buses in the mid-1980s, when deregulation of local bus services forced operators throughout Britain to defend their networks and respond to competition from newly liberated bus companies. In a dramatic move away from high-capacity buses, legions of minibuses seemed to pour on to the streets of towns and cities around the country. The major manufacturers were caught on the hop as operators turned to low-cost, readily available minibuses that were often van conversions, or at best coach-built bodies on light van chassis. Bedford, Dodge (later Renault), Ford, Freight Rover, Mercedes-Benz and Talbot all benefited from a few confusing years when operators exercised their new freedoms, but while some bus companies found an ongoing role for minibuses, others created a demand for something between a minibus and a full-size bus. As such, the midibus was born.

Right: **Deregulation of bus services in Britain, outside London, signalled a move to small and inexpensive minibuses to enable operators to defend their patch and compete for new business. The two minibuses in Berwick-on-Tweed in 1988 are a Lowland Scottish Berwick Beaver Dodge S56 with Alexander 25-seat body and a Northumbria 16-seat Freight Rover. Unlike many minibuses that were van conversions, the Dodge has a coach-built body.**

Below: **Devon was the scene of early minibus activity and here, in 1986, are several multi-coloured 1985 Devon General Ford Transits with Robin Hood converted 16-seat bodies.**

Above: Small vans were the basis of many early minibuses, and this Yorkshire Rider Freight Rover Sherpa with 20-seat Dormobile body is in Hepstonstall in 1995, branded Micro Rider.

Left: Minibuses grew up after the initial excitement of the mid-1980s, like this 2000 Mercedes-Benz O814D with Plaxton 31-seat body working for Crieff Travel in 2004.

The midibus designation had been used before, notably by Seddon, which had produced the Seddon Midi in the early 1970s, very much a scaled-down big bus but with its engine at the front and with bodywork by Seddon's Pennine Coachcraft. It was bought by some of the larger urban fleets but was not quite what the market wanted at that time.

Another promising model that turned out to be ahead of its time was the attractive 24-seat Bedford JJL, with a rear-mounted engine and a stylish body. Just four JJLs were built between 1978 and 1981; this proved to be Bedford's last totally new bus. Bodybuilder Marshall bought the remnants of Bedford's truck business and developed the 8.4m (27ft 6in)-long Minibus, which turned out to be less than reliable.

The Seddon Pennine IV Midi was another attempt to produce a scaled-down full-size bus, in this case a front-engined 25-seater with bodywork by Seddon's in-house builder, Pennine Coachcraft. This 1973 Edinburgh Corporation example was working on hire to Selnec Northern in Bolton when new, between completion at Pennine's premises at nearby Oldham and its journey north.

Bedford launched its attractive JJL midibus model in 1979, and, although it was widely admired, its potential was never realised following Bedford's withdrawal from the UK market. Marshall bought the design rights, which emerged as its less than successful Minibus model. Brighton & Hove was using this 1979 JJL on a city centre shuttle service in Brighton in 1984.

The Marshall Minibus was created from Bedford's JJL, and, while it was arguably a midi rather than minibus, its performance was disappointing. This London General 1996 29-seat example is in service in 1997.

Leyland's offering for the emerging midibus market was the Cub, a front-engined model based on its Terrier truck, and while some mainstream bus operators took examples, it was most successful as a welfare/school bus.

MCW went down a different route in 1986, with its integral front-engined Metrorider model. When MCW stopped bus production in 1989, Optare bought the design and improved it, and the slightly renamed MetroRider went on to enjoy some success.

Dennis developed the sturdy rear-engined Domino midibus in 1985, in many ways a scaled-down version of Dennis' double-deck Dominator chassis and similar to the European idea of a midibus, but only small numbers were sold.

Dennis was more determined when it launched the Dart in 1988, a 9m (29ft 6in)-long rear-engined model with a body built by Duple, which at that time was a fellow Hestair Group company. It struck a chord with bus companies throughout the UK and beyond and went on to become by far the most successful single-deck model produced in recent years, particularly in low-floor form.

Another successful model was the Optare Solo, a neat and adaptable integral bus introduced in 1997 that reimagined midibus design with its entrance behind the front axle. It proved very popular and infinitely adaptable, with wide and narrower versions, and lengths ranging from 7.1m to 10.2m (23ft 3in to 33ft 5in). Rather less successful was the Primo, a 7.9m (25ft 11in)-long midibus mostly built in Hungary from 2005 but completed at Scarborough and badged as a Plaxton model.

Left: This 2006 9.9m (32ft 5in)-long Optare MetroRider 35-seater was in use on Perryman's service between its hometown of Berwick-on-Tweed and Edinburgh.

Below: Another attempt at a scaled-down big bus was the Dennis Domino, a sturdy midi-size chassis with Northern Counties 24-seat body in service with Greater Manchester Transport in 1986; it was new in 1985.

By far the most successful midi-size bus has been the Dennis Dart; this early example, with neat Carlyle 28-seat body, was a demonstrator on hire to the London Buses Metroline company in 1990, seen here against the backdrop of the listed 1932 Arnos Grove underground station. (Tony Wilson)

Right: Another popular model was Optare's innovative rear-engined Solo model, here in 7.2m (23ft 6in)-long 23-seat form working the CityLink service in Liverpool, a 2013 example provided by Cumfybus of Southport.

Below: A less successful small bus was the Plaxton Primo, created from a vehicle imported from Hungary by Enterprise Bus and completed by Plaxton. West Coast Motors operated this new 28-seat Primo in Oban in 2008.

Chapter 7

Rear-engined double-deckers

Introduced in 1956, the double-decker model that broke the mould and was, essentially, the forefather of the majority of double-deckers over the next 40 years was Leyland's rear-engined Atlantean. There had been indications that Leyland's thinking was moving in this direction; two rear-engined prototypes were built in the mid-1950s to test the water, though these were very different from the rear-engined buses that followed.

For a start, they were built to the maximum legal double-deck length of 8.23m (27ft), and the front wheels were right at the front, with the driver separated by a bulkhead from the lower saloon. Passenger access was by a rear entrance, in the style of the great majority of double-deckers in service at the time, but there was one significant difference: the engine was also on the rear platform, Leyland's compact lightly turbocharged O.350 unit.

The 1954 prototype Low Floor Double Deck Bus Chassis (shortened to LFDD) was tested by several potential customers who fed their views back to Leyland. The second prototype was first used by the Glasgow independent operator Lowland Motorways, where it joined the 1954 prototype. By this time, Leyland thinking was influenced by impending relaxation of double-deck length regulations to allow 9.1m (30ft) double-deck buses and the prototype Atlantean was launched in 1956 to a very different specification. Now the entrance was ahead of the front wheels, under control of the driver, and there were seats for an impressive 78 passengers. It had Leyland's big O.600 engine, transversely mounted across the rear. It had an impressively low overall height, just 4.04m (13ft 3in), even though most customers were happy with the 4.42m (14ft 6in) height of most urban buses.

The second of Leyland's rear-engined double-deck prototypes is now preserved and in the North West Museum of Road Transport in St Helens. It was built in 1955 and received a rear entrance 63-seat Metro-Cammell body – the engine was mounted on the rear platform. The frontal arrangement is interesting and is reminiscent of London Transport's pre-war TF class Leylands.

Leyland liked the idea of selling complete integrally built buses, and the 1956 Atlantean prototype was an integral with low-height Metro-Cammell bodywork. Bus operators liked the idea of the Atlantean but not as an integral. They wanted to specify their own bodies from their regular suppliers, so Leyland went back and developed the Atlantean as a separate chassis, which was launched in 1958. Some operators were initially cautious, but gradually Atlanteans were appearing in many of the largest fleets.

For operators with low bridge problems, Leyland and Metro-Cammell had evolved an awkward semi-lowbridge upper deck layout that gave a seating capacity of 73, although 16 of these seats were on four-across seats on the upper deck accessed from a short nearside gangway. This situation put Daimler at an advantage when it introduced its new Fleetline chassis, as it used a drop-centre rear axle to provide a flat lower deck floor, which enabled bodybuilders to construct low-height bodies with normal seating on both decks on the chassis.

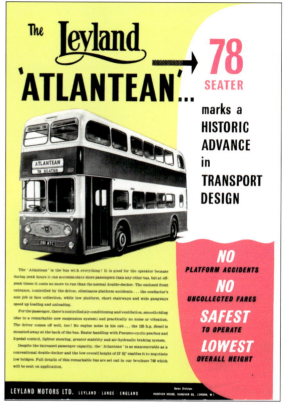

Above right: **This early advert for Leyland's Atlantean featured this 1956 prototype integral bus that was demonstrated to operators around the UK. Although production Atlanteans would be different, the copywriter was not wrong with the words that the Atlantean 'marks a historic advance in transport design'.**

Below: **Although early Atlanteans tended to go to the larger fleets, independent operators also took delivery of new examples, like Cunningham's of Paisley with this AN68 model with 76-seat Roe body, new in 1977.**

Hot on the heels of the Atlantean came Daimler's Fleetline, which offered a Gardner engine and a proper low-height chassis. Coventry Corporation supported local industry when it bought the Fleetline, and this 1973 bus is still in Coventry colours in 1977, although that undertaking was transferred to West Midlands PTE in 1974. It has East Lancs 74-seat bodywork.

The next competitor was Bristol, with its VRT chassis in 1968, but, by this time, the former bus manufacturing rivals AEC, Bristol, Daimler, Guy and Leyland were all bedfellows under the monolith that was British Leyland. With British Leyland's inheritance of three rear-engined double-deck chassis – the Bristol VRT, Daimler Fleetline and Leyland Atlantean – it was clear that at least one of these would have to go, and as it turned out the Atlantean was the survivor, helped by a major 1972 revamp that eliminated many of its weak points.

The Bristol VRT was developed for state-owned operators, but three years before its 1968 launch, Bristol and ECW products had become generally available, and the VRT was specified by a wider range of customers. This 1977 74-seat example was new to Southdown, passing into the separated Brighton & Hove fleet in 1985 in preparation for privatisation.

British Leyland's grand plan was to replace the three inherited rear-engined double-deck models with one full-height integral model, which materialised as the B15, later Titan, in 1975. This was not a popular move, though the Titan became a successful London model, in spite of suffering from more than its fair share of production and relocation problems.

And there were more problems for Leyland. Other manufacturers, concerned by Leyland's apparent monopoly, saw an opportunity to develop and build competing models. In 1973, Scania and MCW combined to produce the Metropolitan, a powerful rear-engined double-decker, while the Volvo Ailsa reinvented the concept of the front-engined double-decker. Then came the Dennis Dominator in 1977, followed by the MCW Metrobus in 1979. For a few years, the Titan and Metrobus shared London's double-deck orders.

Right: Leyland planned to replace its ageing triumvirate of rear-engined double-deckers – the Atlantean, Fleetline and VRT – with a new standard model, known initially by its codename B15. This advanced model was to be an all-Leyland product, aimed primarily at the London market, but other operators were unhappy, and Leyland appeased them with the more straightforward (and ultimately more successful) Olympian. This is one of the prototype B15s in Coventry, at the 1978 launch when the model name Titan was revealed – note the small Titan badge under the word Leyland.

Below: Operators were unhappy about Leyland's apparent monopoly of the double-deck market, and newcomers were encouraged to fill the gap. The Metropolitan was a joint venture between Scania and MCW and larger fleets bought some, including London Transport and, as seen here, Tyne & Wear PTE. This is a 1977 76-seater.

Dennis saw an opportunity to sell double-deckers to operators who had previously bought Leyland's Fleetline and introduced the Dominator, which sold well with a choice of Gardner or Rolls-Royce engines. This Brighton Borough Transport 1985 Dominator has 74-seat East Lancs bodywork.

The MCW Metrobus and the Leyland (later Volvo) Olympian were the most successful of the last generation of step-entry double-deckers. Most Metrobuses were complete MCW vehicles, but the underframe was bodied by other builders, and Alexander built low-height RL-bodied Metrobuses for Midland Scottish. This 1985 78-seat example is in Stirling in 1997, in First Midland Bluebird livery following SBG privatisation.

The growing presence of chassis imported from mainland Europe brought new double-deck models to the UK market – the Scania N series in 1980, and the DAF DB250 and Iveco TurboCity, both in 1991. DAF and Scania would persevere with the UK double-deck market, going on to produce low-floor versions of their step-entrance models from 1998 onwards.

Leyland's Atlantean was showing its age after more than 20 years in production and so, in 1980, it introduced the Olympian, which proved popular for 13 years as a Leyland model, then for another five years as a Volvo model, following Volvo's acquisition of Leyland Bus in 1988.

Right: Scania came into the UK with double-deck models in its own right in 1980; this is a 1996 N113DRB model with 76-seat East Lancs body supplied to Mayne of Manchester.

Below: Optare developed a reputation for attractive buses, and the Spectra, on DAF DB250 chassis, introduced a softer look that other bodybuilders sought to adopt. This 74-seat Spectra was new to Reading Buses in 1994 and is seen here in 2007.

In the late 1990s, the writing was on the wall for step-entrance double-deckers. Following the enthusiastic adoption of low-floor single-deckers, there were moves to design and produce double-deck equivalents, and as these followed from 1998; popular models like the Olympian gave way to a completely new double-decker breed. Though, there was one last step-entrance double-deck model, just as thoughts were turning to low-floor types – the Dennis Arrow, based on Dennis' single-deck Lance chassis.

For its low-cost Magic Bus network in Manchester, Stagecoach used three-axle Leyland Olympians with 94-seat Alexander bodies re-imported from Citybus in Hong Kong. This well-filled example, new in 1990, is in service in Manchester in 2007.

Following the Volvo acquisition of Leyland Bus, the Olympian continued in production as a reworked Volvo model. Lothian was an enthusiastic Olympian customer, and this is a late-model (1996) Volvo example with Alexander Royale 80-seat body, here pursued by a similar bus in the First Edinburgh fleet.

A late arrival on the pre-low-floor double-deck scene was the Dennis Arrow, introduced in 1997. This 77-seat East Lancs-bodied Arrow for Capital Citybus in London was new in 1997. (Tony Wilson)

Chapter 8

Rear-engined single-deckers

Bristol broke the mould in 1962 with an 11m (36ft)-long rear-engined chassis, the RE. From a company that had built its reputation on producing sturdy, reliable but often unexciting buses, it claimed two 'firsts' in under 15 years. First, in 1949, it had introduced the low-height Lodekka, described earlier in this book, and now came the RE, the first successful production rear-engined single-deck model for the UK market. Other chassis followed from the usual suspects, but many agree that the RE was the best of the bunch.

The RE set a pattern that was quickly copied, with a horizontal engine under the floor at the rear enabling maximum seating space. Other chassis also came along with vertical engines, some mounted transversely across the rear and others with compact units in-line with the chassis.

Initially, the Bristol RE was available only to state-owned fleets and was bought in substantial numbers by the Tilling and Scottish groups. After the Leyland–Bristol share exchange in 1965, which brought Bristol chassis back on to the open market for the first time in 17 years, it was bought by BET Group and municipal fleets, and remained in production for Ulsterbus as an 'export' customer after

The Bristol RE was the first and, as it turned out, the best of the first-generation rear-engined single-deck models. Designed for state-owned fleets, it found ready customers throughout the UK and beyond when Bristol and ECW products became generally available. Hartlepool Corporation tried a number of single-deck models, including the RE. This RELL6L model with two-door ECW 46-seat body was new in 1975.

Bristol's successful RELL chassis was kept in production for Citybus and Ulsterbus in Northern Ireland after it was no longer available for customers in mainland Britain, who Leyland hoped would buy the new Leyland National model. This 1980 Citybus RELL6G in Belfast has 32-seat bodywork by Alexander (Belfast).

British Leyland's other rear-engined single-deckers disappeared from the model lists to stimulate sales of the Leyland National.

Several builders had explored the possibility of moving bus engines from the front to the back. Leyland had built a rear-engined prototype in the 1930s and Midland Red had experimented in the 1930s and 1940s for its own fleet. However, in the 1950s, the only production rear-engined single-deck model came from truck builder Foden, which attempted to break into the bus and coach market in the 1940s. The Foden PVRF6 offered a Foden diesel engine as standard with the option of the engineers' favourite Gardner 6LW. These were big engines, mounted transversely across the rear of the chassis and, while most examples sold were for coach rather than bus work, it was not a sales success. The market, it seemed, was not quite ready for rear-mounted engines.

The Bristol RE changed all that after it first appeared in 1962, and it was quickly followed from the British Leyland stable by the AEC Swift/Merlin range, the Daimler Roadliner and the Leyland Panther and Panther Cub models. None of these achieved anything like the popularity of the RE. London Transport famously bought substantial batches of the AEC models, which proved to be less than satisfactory for London conditions and had short service lives there. The Panther and the shorter Panther Cub had some success, but Daimler's Roadliner was widely regarded as a brave concept that was let down by the choice of an unfamiliar engine.

Daimler's reputation as a bus builder was earned by a succession of well-engineered chassis, usually with the tried and tested Gardner range of engines. For its Roadliner, Daimler chose the compact Cummins V6-200, a unit largely unknown in the UK, and this proved to be its Achilles' heel, as its performance and reliability were disappointing. In a last-ditch attempt to salvage the Roadliner, Daimler offered a Perkins V8 engine, but it was too late to save the model's reputation. Daimler's contemporary double-deck offering was the popular rear-engined Fleetline, and to try and win some business back, a single-deck version was produced, sold on a premise of fleet standardisation.

The newly created London Country company experimented with rear-engined single-deck models in the early 1970s. At Stevenage in 1972 are three buses in the Stevenage SuperBus livery – a 1971 AEC Swift/MCW in the centre, flanked on the left by a very early Leyland National and on the right by a Metro-Scania. The buses were new in 1971 and 1972.

Leyland's rear-engined single-decker offering was the Panther. Preston Corporation supported its local manufacturer, and this is a 1973 Panther with 48-seat Pennine bodywork in Preston's iconic bus station in 1984, promoting the Red Rose Rambler bus ticket.

The Roadliner was Daimler's contribution to the new wave of rear-engined single-deckers, but it proved to be an unreliable bus in service, and few were built. This 1967 Roadliner with 54-seat Strachans body is now preserved at The Transport Museum at Wythall. (Sholto Thomas)

After the disappointment of the Roadliner, Daimler offered a single-deck version of its successful Fleetline double-decker, selling it on the premise of fleet standardisation. This 1970 Fleetline SRG with Marshall 45-seat body was new to Maidstone & District in 1970 and is seen here working for East Kent at Dover in 1978, in Sealink colours.

This enjoyed some success, but the chunky upright Gardner engine at the back reduced the available space for passengers, where other rear-engined single-deckers had more compact units mounted under the floor, and could also cause structural problems for bodybuilders and operators.

For SBG companies, Albion developed the Viking VK43 model, as a simple rear-engined chassis for lighter duties, mainly to replace the fleets of older front-engined buses. SBG was the main customer for the Viking VK43, with Alexander bus and coach bodywork.

Then, in 1972, the Leyland National appeared, a joint venture between British Leyland and the National Bus Company and very much a mould-breaker. It was a complete integral bus available in 10.3m and 11.3m (33ft 9in and 37ft) lengths and built on a production line installed at a new-build plant at Workington in Cumbria. Up to that time, single-deck buses typically consisted of a chassis, hand-built in say Southall in London or Leyland in Lancashire, then driven to a bodybuilder that could typically be anywhere between Park Royal in London and Falkirk in Stirlingshire. The mechanical specification of the chassis would be agreed between the operator and the builder, and the body would be to suit the customer's requirements internally and externally.

That was not the case with the National, which came as a largely standard bus, even to the choice of colour. Not quite Henry Ford's description of the initial colour choices for his Model T Ford: 'any colour – so long as it's black'; the National choice was slightly wider: any colour – so long as it is red or green. Workington was an assembly plant, with very little constructed on the premises but with all major mechanical and body components shipped in for assembly on the slow-moving line. The National looked unlike any previous single-decker and was unashamedly a bus, with a relatively low floorline and up to 52 seats. One advantage was that it could be supplied quicker than conventional body-on-chassis buses, and this proved to be an attraction for some operators. However, some resented

The SBG was not drawn to the Leyland National initially, but delivery problems with its normal suppliers led to orders for the easily available National. This is a Mk1 52-seater supplied to Fife Scottish, in Kirkcaldy when new in 1978.

The life of some Leyland Nationals was prolonged following refurbishment by East Lancs to create the Leyland National Greenway, retaining the structure but updating the appearance. Mainline in Sheffield was operating this 1979 example, which had been rebuilt as a Greenway in 1992.

the fact that Leyland had stopped building its other rear-engined chassis and they started to look elsewhere. Though, at first there was not really an 'elsewhere' to look. British Leyland was virtually the only show in town – or so it must have appeared.

However, other manufacturers saw an opening by introducing new models that they thought would appeal to disaffected Leyland customers. Seddon, a minor player in the UK bus market, introduced the Pennine RU in 1969, with a rear-mounted Gardner engine aimed at fleets that would normally have bought the Bristol RE; just over 270 were built over the next five years. Then, MCW linked with Scania to produce the Metro-Scania, a UK-assembled version of Scania's sophisticated Swedish-built BR110, but with limited success; only 120 were sold between 1970 and 1973. Mercedes-Benz and Volvo also tested the water with rear-engined bus chassis in the 1970s. However, that decade belonged to the Leyland National, which was relaunched in 1979 as the slightly longer National 2, with what most engineers would regard as 'proper' bus engines, Leyland units inevitably but as a concession, the Gardner 6HLXB was also offered. Although there had always been resistance among some operators about the lack of choice when the National was introduced, more than 7,700 were built in its 13-year production run.

By the early 1980s, other builders recognised opportunities to develop new rear-engined single-deck models. Dennis, long-established as a bus chassis builder, had introduced the Dominator double-deck chassis in 1977 to fill the gap left by Leyland's Fleetline and had seen an opportunity for a single-deck Dominator in 1978. This then led to introduction of the Falcon H and HC models with a horizontal Gardner 6HLXB at the rear – essentially, the Bristol RE reborn yet again.

The Seddon RU was designed to offer operators a Gardner-engined model. Fylde Borough was operating this 1972 Pennine-bodied 47-seater in St Annes in 1982.

The Metro-Scania introduced UK operators to Scania buses at a time when Selnec PTE was trying various experimental (EX) types before deciding on the standard types for its fleet. The Metro-Scania was essentially a Swedish-built Scania BR111 completed by MCW in the UK and gained a reputation for its powerful engine. In Manchester in 1973, bus EX47 would easily beat the Austin taxi away from the traffic lights.

SBG went on to buy the revamped and bigger-engined Leyland National 2, distinguished from the earlier model by its front-mounted radiator and more rounded front. This 1980 Highland Scottish 52-seater is seen in Inverness in 1984.

Hartlepool was sampling different single-deck models in the 1970s. In addition to the Bristol RELL, it tried the single-decker Dennis Dominator in 1979, here with a slightly ungainly East Lancs 43-seat body in 1980, as well as Dennis Falcons, Leyland Nationals and Volvo B10Ms.

Dennis answered the call for a Gardner-engined model with the Falcon H. This Hyndburn 1984 delivery, here in 1989, has a fairly high-built East Lancs 44-seat body.

Darlington had bought other rear-engined single-deckers but commissioned Huddersfield-based Ward Motors to develop an equivalent Gardner-engined chassis. The Ward Dalesman GRXI was the result, and just six were built in 1983, with Wadham Stringer 46-seat bodies, as photographed here in 1991. GRXI stood for Gardner Rear 11m (Roman numerals).

Now there were changes coming that would cause ripples for decades to come. First was the deregulation of express coach services in 1980, and what many had regarded as the inevitable deregulation of bus services in 1986. Bus and coach companies used to a market that had been tightly regulated since the 1930 Road Traffic Act now had to learn to compete and how to respond to competition. At the same time, the National Bus Company was being privatised. All these events had a knock-on effect for the bus and coach builders who were watching to see what would happen to the market for new vehicles. On the bus side, many operators erred on the side of caution and held back from major investment in the big buses they had been using to stock their fleets.

In order that they could compete and defend their territory, many bus operators turned to minibuses – cheap to buy and cheap to run when cost-cutting and competitive fare-cutting were on the agenda. As the 1980s progressed, this trend threatened the long-term future of long-established bus builders, and the line-up of operators and suppliers in 1990 looked very different from the 1980 situation.

Although the market for full-size rear-engined single-deckers would shrink, there were still new models appearing. The Leyland National had enjoyed its second wind in big-engined National 2 form but Leyland replaced it in 1985 – not the best year to introduce a model of this type – with the Lynx, a semi-integral city bus built at the Workington plant. Optare started with some double-decker bodies and some attractive smaller buses before launching the Delta, a stylish full-size single-decker on DAF SB220 chassis. Around the same time, as previously mentioned, a new model appeared that would go on to be one of the best-selling buses of all time: the Dennis Dart.

Where once operators would have chosen a heavyweight single-deck type, the Dart changed all that, but there was still a demand for big-engined full-size buses. Volvo introduced the B10B into the UK market in 1992, Mercedes-Benz the O405 in the same year and Scania had been nibbling at the UK market since the mid-1980s.

The successor to the Leyland National was the semi-integral Lynx, launched in 1985 just as the bus industry was in turmoil with imminent deregulation and larger buses went briefly out of fashion. These two 49-seat Lynxes were delivered in 1987 for Shearings routes in Greater Manchester.

Marketed as the Optare Delta, this stylish single-deck design built on DAF SB220 chassis represented a breakaway from the squarer outline of many buses of the time. A 1989 48-seat delivery in the interesting livery of the Northumbria company is in service here in 1994.

Volvo's rear-engined offering was the B10B, replacing Leyland's Lynx, and it sold to a range of operators, including independents like Hutchison of Overtown; this is a newly delivered 1993 example with 51-seat Northern Counties body.

Alexander offered its Strider body on the Volvo B10B chassis, like this brand-new Harrogate & District 49-seater in Leeds in 1995.

Mercedes-Benz sold into the UK market with its O405 model, fitted with bodies by a range of builders. This 1997 O405 for First Aberdeen combines the Mercedes front end with a Wrights Endurance 49-seat body.

Midland Bluebird bought this Scania N113CRB with Wrights Endurance 49-seat body in 1994, photographed when new in Edinburgh.

Although most UK operators recognised the importance of making their buses accessible for as many passengers as possible, single-deckers like the Lynx and Delta still had shallow steps at the entrance – admittedly, though, these were fewer and shallower than the often-awkward entrances on some underfloor-engined single-deckers. Operators in mainland Europe were already taking the first examples of a new breed of low-floor single-deck bus, and the UK would follow.

Early Wrights-bodied buses on Dennis Dart chassis in the London fleets had the slightly retro Handybus design. This was one of 14 supplied to the Westlink operation, which ended up with London United, here approaching its terminus in Esher in 1999.

Chapter 9
Articulated single-deckers

In many parts of the world, articulated single-deckers provide the capacity that UK operators achieve with double-deckers, although there are still pockets of high-capacity double-deckers beyond the UK. Artic single-deckers usually provide a minimum of seats and a considerable amount of standing space. Bus passengers in the UK have got used to getting a seat, so artics have had mixed success in the UK.

In the 1970s, manufacturers from mainland Europe tried to tempt UK customers by sending artic demonstrators across for operators to examine, and an early convert was South Yorkshire PTE (SYPTE), looking for buses for city services in Sheffield where passengers were typically making short journeys. In 1977, Leyland imported an 18m (59ft)-long left-hand drive artic built by DAB, and this was given dispensation for a three-day trial in passenger-carrying service in Sheffield.

In 1978, SYPTE bought five right-hand drive MAN artics, and these were followed in 1979 by five Leyland-DAB artics with British-built bodywork using Leyland National parts. These were used on a free circular service in Sheffield, but they were returned to their manufacturers in 1981.

The first artics for SYPTE were Leyland/DAB models, using a Danish DAB chassis and a Leyland National-based 60-seat body. This 1979 example had been sold to McGill's of Barrhead and is in Glasgow in 1983.

Later SYPTE artics were complete Leyland/DAB models, and this 1985 61-seater is in Greenwich in 1992, on hire to the London Buses Selkent company to gain experience of artics. (Tony Wilson)

SYPTE also bought MAN SG192R 63-seat artics in 1978, and this one is in service in Sheffield in 1980.

South Yorkshire Transport (SYPTE's successor) returned for 13 more Leyland-DAB artics in 1985, and these lasted in service in Sheffield and Rotherham with the privatised Mainline company until 1999.

In the meantime, Grampian Regional Transport bought a single Mercedes-Benz O405G artic in 1992. Grampian was an important component of what became FirstGroup, and outside London the group invested heavily in artics for its Aberdeen, Bath, Glasgow, Greater Manchester, Leeds, York and Dublin fleets. Most were Volvo B7LA and B10BLA models with Wrights bodywork, and there were Scania L94UAs with Wrights and Scania bodies, and Mercedes-Benz Citaros.

The privatised Grampian company, which would become a major component of the new FirstGroup, bought this Mercedes-Benz O405G with Alexander 61-seat body in 1992. First would go on to invest in low-floor artics.

Nottingham City Transport displayed this 2001 Wrights-bodied Scania L9UA 59-seat artic to the public in the city centre when it was newly delivered.

Cardiff was another municipal operator to favour artics, and this is a 2006 Scania N94UA 53-seater in service when new.

FirstBus allocated artics to some of its city fleets. In service with First Aberdeen in 2014 is this 2000 Volvo B7LA with 56-seat Wrights body, complete with spat-like covers on the second and third axles. The streetscape confirms Aberdeen's nickname of the Granite City.

London operators bought nearly 400 Mercedes-Benz Citaro artics between 2002 and 2005, but implied concerns about safety led to their premature withdrawal; all had gone by 2011, which paved the way for Boris Johnson's New Routemaster double-decker. Other UK fleets investing in artics were Cardiff (Scania OmniCity), Travel West Midlands (Mercedes-Benz O405 and Citaro), and Citybus in Northern Ireland (Mercedes-Benz).

FirstGroup reinvented the artic with the StreetCar, developed for First by Volvo and Wrights. Thirty-eight were built in 2006/2007 for operations in Leeds, Swansea and York.

Articulated coaches have been considered for UK duties, and Stagecoach took the plunge and bought Volvo B10MA models in the 1990s, with Jonckheere and Plaxton bodies for interurban work.

Left: London operators famously bought almost 400 Mercedes-Benz 49-seat Citaro O530G artics between 2002 and 2005. This is a Stagecoach Selkent example, photographed when new in 2003, appropriately in the company of a Mercedes-Benz car as it circumnavigates Trafalgar Square.

Below: The ultimate FirstBus artic was the StreetCar, a fresh re-thinking of the artic concept by Wrights using a modified Volvo B7LA underframe. This 2007 37-seat example is in service in Leeds when new in 2007.

Chapter 10
Low-floor single-deckers

T he move towards fully accessible low-floor single-deckers had started in mainland Europe and UK operators were closely watching this trend. The first low-floors came at a premium price, which was not always a problem for heavily subsidised European operators but was perceived as a barrier to their widespread use in the UK. However, in September 1992, Merseytravel, the Merseyside PTE, brought four models into the UK to show what was possible – a Den Oudsten Alliance, an MAN NL202, a Neoplan N4014 and a Van Hool A300.

London Buses was the first UK operator to place a significant order for low-floor single-deckers – 38 Dennis Lance SLF and 30 Scania N113CRL, all with bodies by Wrights. Other European builders came along with offerings for the UK market – the Scania MaxCi and the Volvo B10L and B10BLE – but the market really opened up when Dennis introduced the SLF (Super Low Floor) version of its best-selling Dart. This gave operators an affordable model available in a number of lengths, from large midis to virtually full-size buses.

Among the first low-floor single-deckers to enter service in the UK were German-built Neoplan N4016 33-seaters for Merseytravel in 1994, and this one is in Liverpool in 1996. (Tony Wilson)

The first low-floor bus to operate in Scotland was this 1993 Scania N113CRL with East Lancs 42-seat body for Tayside, here when new with an appropriate registration number.

Most UK-built chassis have been strictly low-*entry* buses, with the low floor area stretching from the entrance to a point ahead of the rear axle, where steps take passengers to the rear of the saloon, sometimes at a much higher level. Chassis like this are less expensive to build and simpler to maintain than fully low-floor models favoured in mainland Europe. Some of these have entered service in the UK, but manufacturers have responded to the UK's preferences and developed a range of low-entry types. The continental preference for multi-doored urban buses requires a flat gangway, but seating is usually mounted on platforms rising from the floor.

Dennis' Dart dominated the single-deck bus market for years, and a reduced demand for heavyweight types was mainly catered for by Volvo with its B7L, B7RLE and B8RLE, DAF with the SB220 and Scania with variations of its N, K and L series models. Other manufacturers cast envious eyes on the runaway success of Dennis' Dart and DAF came up with the SB120 and Volvo the B6LE. A mixed bag of European builders exported to the UK, with varying degrees of success; Irisbus and Neoplan sold small numbers, while MAN and Mercedes-Benz enjoyed good sales. MAN offered a wide range of chassis and was most successful with its 18.220 model, which was bought in substantial numbers by Stagecoach. The Mercedes-Benz O405N and its successor, the Citaro, have sold well in the UK and we have seen that the O530G Citaro was famously chosen by London operators for the controversial and short-lived dalliance with articulated buses.

Over the years, the distinction between full-size heavyweight and lighter-weight chassis has become blurred. Where European manufacturers like Mercedes-Benz, Scania and Volvo have produced heavier buses for their home markets, and have sold successfully to UK operators, the domestic manufacturers have tended to offer light/medium weight models.

The Dennis Dart SLF quickly became the most successful low-floor model. This is a 2001 Transdev London United 30-seat SLF with Plaxton Pointer body in Surbiton in 2009.

A Stagecoach Western 1997 Volvo B6LE with Alexander ALX200 36-seat body in Glasgow when new, proclaiming itself to be a 'new super low floor easy access bus'.

A 2007 VDL SB200 with Plaxton Centro 45-seat body in Preston in 2015, operating for the fondly remembered independent John Fishwick & Sons of Leyland. DAF models adopted the VDL name from 2003.

A newly delivered Scania N113CRL with 45-seat East Lancs body in service in Paisley in 1995 with the privatised Clydeside 2000 company.

The first buses Arriva Kent Thameside operated on the innovative Fastrack services between Dartford and the Bluewater shopping centre were Volvo B7RLEs with Wrights Eclipse 40-seat bodies, bought in 2006. This one is at the Dartford terminus when new.

Stagecoach was the major UK customer for the MAN 18.220 chassis and most carried Alexander ALX300 42-seat bodies, like this 2001 Stagecoach Cambridge example in 2009.

A 2015 Cardiff Bus 41-seat Mercedes-Benz Citaro O530 in central Cardiff in 2018. The Citaro has sold in great numbers throughout the world.

The phenomenal success of the Dennis Dart and its direct successor, the ADL Enviro200, is testimony to the adaptability of the chassis. First conceived as a step-entrance midi-size bus, in SLF form, it has proved to be remarkably flexible, responding to the varying needs of bus operators.

This prototype Alexander Dennis Enviro200 is on trial with Metroline in London's Highgate Village in 2005. It was unusual with its second door positioned behind the rear wheels, and production examples featured a different front end and rear engine layout. (Tony Wilson)

The Alexander Dennis Enviro300 was introduced as a full-length lightweight bus. This First Edinburgh 2013 41-seat delivery is in Galashiels in 2018.

The best-selling Alexander Dennis Enviro200 is popular with London operators. This London General 2007 E200 is in Wimbledon when new.

Other manufacturers recognised the attraction of lighter models. Optare offered its Excel, Tempo, Versa and Metrocity in a range of lengths, and even the popular Solo could be stretched to a very long-wheelbase 10.2m (33ft 5in) version. VDL, previously DAF, offered its adaptable SB120, SB180 and SB200 models.

The Wrights offering was the StreetLite, like its competitors an adaptable integral model available in two forms – wheel forward (WF) with the entrance behind the front wheels, and door forward (DF) with the door ahead of them. The WF model is available in lengths between 8.8m and 9.5m (28ft 10in and 31ft 2in), and the DF in a wider range, from 9.6m to 11.5m (31ft 5in to 37ft 7in). It is also available with micro hybrid technology, and under the reconstituted Wrights business, has gained the Ultroliner name.

Left: Optare produced a range of low-floor single-deck models; this is a 2017 40-seat Metrocity working for Borders Buses, here in central Edinburgh in 2018.

Below: The Wrights StreetLite is a midi-size integral produced in a range of lengths. This Stagecoach Western 2015 StreetLite DF 37-seater on a Strathclyde tendered service passes Lochranza Castle on the island of Arran in 2019.

Chapter 11

Low-floor
double-deckers

The enthusiastic switch to low-floor single-deckers in the 1990s prompted calls for low-floor *double*-deckers as well. Where many of the single-deck models were already well established in mainland Europe, there had been no real market for the double-deckers that had always been popular in the UK. European bus builders like DAF, Scania and Volvo were already selling single-deck buses and coaches into UK fleets, and DAF recognised the opportunity to combine elements of chassis already in production to produce a low-floor double-decker for UK consumption. DAF was already selling step-entry DB250 double-deckers to UK operators, and a low-floor chassis was launched late in 1995. The first low-floor double-decker to enter service was a DB250LF with Optare Spectra body delivered early in 1998 to the independent operator Abus of Bristol; DAF's pioneering efforts won it some useful orders and also spurred other main players like Dennis, Scania and Volvo to design and produce their equivalent models.

An interesting bus was on display at the Coach & Bus '97 show. It only proclaimed itself the Plaxton President, which was the body style and the prototype of many more that would enter service over the

The first low-floor double-decker to enter service in the UK was this 81-seat Optare-bodied DAF DB250 of Abus of Bristol, new in 1998, and seen here in March 2011 in Cheltenham. (Sholto Thomas)

next few years. Closer inspection revealed that the chassis was a Volvo, a version of its B7L European model. Volvo had been the clear market leader with its step-entry Olympian chassis, but UK buyers were not convinced by its in-line nearside-mounted rear engine and long rear overhang. UK buyers had shown a preference for transversely mounted rear engines on their double-deckers, so Volvo had to go back to basics and came up with the highly successful B7TL chassis in 1999.

This delay enabled Dennis, now a mainstream volume bus builder, to steal a march on its Swedish rival with its Trident in 1998, and the Trident developed into the Enviro400, which in turn has spawned hybrid, electric and projected hydrogen versions.

Left: Brighton & Hove was an early customer for the Dennis Trident. This 2000 example with East Lancs 78-seat body is at Brighton railway station in 2005.

Below: Stagecoach built up a substantial fleet of Tridents with Alexander ALX400 bodies around the UK, including many for its London operations. This 2003 Trident 68-seater from Stagecoach's East London fleet heads towards the Strand in 2008.

The Alexander Dennis Enviro400 succeeded the Trident, and this is a 2013 'more' branded Wilts & Dorset 79-seater in Bournemouth in 2019.

Volvo's diesel chassis followed a similar path, with the successive B7TL, B9TL and B5TL models and the three-axle B8L, as well as the hybrid B5LH and the more recently announced electric BZL.

DAF (later VDL), Dennis and Volvo faced competition from Scania, which had sold step-entry double-deckers into the UK market and returned to this sector with its OmniDekka model in 2003, joined by the OmniCity in 2005 and diesel and gas-powered N-series models from 2006. The OmniDekka was a joint venture with East Lancs bodywork, and the OmniCity was an all-Scania product. Later N-series chassis have been bodied by East Lancs and Alexander Dennis.

Wrights was a latecomer to the double-deck market. It had won substantial single-deck orders from all parts of the UK and in 2001 introduced its Gemini double-deck body, which quickly became familiar on DAF/VDL and Volvo chassis. Like Alexander Dennis, its main rival for the UK double-deck market, Wrights was increasingly moving from building bodies on chassis supplied by giants like Volvo and was creating its own range of complete integrally built models. It moved into producing complete double-deckers from 2007, with diesel-electric hybrid models aimed largely at the London bus market, and it also successfully won the contract to build the 1,000 New Buses for London – the New Routemaster hybrid – between 2012 and 2018. There was also the 2DL, built by Wrights using a VDL chassis module, and largely found in London service.

The Volvo B7TL was a popular model throughout the UK, many with Wrights Gemini bodies, like this 2003 Go-Ahead London 64-seater in Whitehall in 2013.

Left: The Volvo B9TL replaced the B7TL from 2006 and continued its sales success. This First Edinburgh 2007 B9TL with Wrights 74-seat body is typical of many supplied to FirstBus fleets. It is in Peebles in 2012.

Below: Volvo's B9TL was replaced by the B5TL and this Yellow Buses 2015 example with 73-seat Wrights Gemini 3 bodywork is in Bournemouth in 2015.

Lothian Buses introduced a fleet of 100-seat Volvo B8Ls with Alexander Dennis 400XLB bodies in 2019. Similar three-axle buses, but with two fewer seats, have also been built for Stagecoach use on the Cambridge guided busway.

Right: In addition to supplying low-floor double-deck chassis, Scania introduced a complete model in 2005, the OmniCity with Polish-built Scania body. This one for Southern Vectis, the Isle of Wight operator, is a 2008 76-seater, in Newport in 2009.

Below: A 2010 Oxford Bus Scania N230UD with Alexander Dennis 76-seat body leaves Oxford railway station in 2012.

The Wrights Gemini 2 DL was a semi-integral model based on the VDL DB300 chassis and was mainly built for Arriva companies. This 2009 example is an Arriva London 65-seater in High Holborn in 2014.

The Wrights Gemini 2 was also produced in low-height form, hence the flatter roof profile. Arriva Merseyside operated this 2011 70-seater, seen here in Liverpool in 2012.

Wrights moved decisively into the integral double-deck market with the introduction of the StreetDeck in 2014, a model that has proved popular with some of the larger groups. After a change of ownership in 2019, Wrights bounced back with a revised and renamed double-deck range. The StreetDeck EU6 Ultroliner is the diesel offering, the StreetDeck Electroliner BEV is the battery electric model, and the StreetDeck Hydroliner FCEV is the world's first production hydrogen double-decker.

Optare, which had built itself a reputation for innovative and stylish buses, bodied early DAF DB250LF models and returned to the double-deck market in 2014 with a handful of diesel-engined Metrodeckers, before it re-emerged as a full electric version the following year.

Increasing concerns about the effect of vehicle emissions on climate change has led to significant changes in double-deck design. The move to EuroVI standards from 2013 has encouraged manufacturers to develop a new generation of cleaner diesel double-deckers and branch into other alternatives.

Wrights' integral StreetDeck model was introduced in 2014. This is a Reading 2016 70-seater in 2018. It features the glazed staircase panels that became popular following their first appearance on London's New Routemaster.

Chapter 12

Towards zero emissions

The diesel engine has served the bus industry well from its introduction and widespread adoption in the 1930s, and is still in favour with many operators, particularly in its ultra-clean Euro VI form. The European Union emission standards started with Euro I in the early 1990s and increasingly stringent requirements brought us to Euro VI from 2013. However, manufacturers were working on alternatives – hydrogen fuel-cell buses, a new generation of gas buses, hybrid diesel-electric buses and battery-powered electric buses.

There was nothing new about using gas or electricity to power buses. At the end of the 19th century, when the first electric tramways were being introduced in UK towns and cities, it seemed reasonable to some that battery-powered road vehicles would follow. There were some early experiments, rendered quickly obsolete by the arrival of the first petrol-engined buses.

The concept of electric buses never really went away. Trolleybuses, requiring no rails but drawing power from overhead wires, were a popular municipal option in the UK, particularly when the same municipality generated the electricity; the first UK trolleybuses operated in 1911 and the last examples in 1972.

However, there were still stirrings of interest in battery-powered buses, from a 1972 Department of Trade and Industry-sponsored experiment to buses built for Selnec (South-East Lancashire, North-East Cheshire) PTE and a Leyland National towing its batteries in a trailer. These experiments helped

Trolleybuses were a popular alternative to petrol and diesel buses, as well as trams, in the early part of the 20th century, often using municipally provided electricity, but the last UK trolleybuses were withdrawn in 1972. A revived interest resulted in this experimental 1985 Dennis Dominator trolleybus with Alexander 80-seat body, built as a demonstration vehicle in 1985 for South Yorkshire, and here in preservation in 2000 at the Trolleybus Museum at Sandtoft in Lincolnshire. (Tony Wilson)

manufacturers and operators to understand the advantages and disadvantages of this mode, and there were often more disadvantages owing to battery size and weight and, important for bus companies, range.

Gas buses were born out of the necessity to conserve conventional fuel during the two world wars – coal gas in large balloons on the roof of single-deck buses in World War One and producer gas trailers in World War Two. Liquid Petroleum Gas (LPG) was briefly used experimentally in the 1970s with gas engines fitted to a few rear-engined double-deckers, but fuel consumption was poor and fuel costs were higher than in equivalent diesel models.

Gas buses never really went away, and Scania has persevered with single-deck and double-deck chassis powered by Compressed Natural Gas (CNG) or Biomethane, working with Alexander Dennis.

Right: Another experiment with electric traction was this 1973 former Ribble Leyland National, which was converted in 1974 to tow a trailer containing its batteries. It was used briefly by Crosville on the Runcorn Busway.

Below: Scania has persevered with biogas models, and Nottingham has been an enthusiastic customer. This is a 2019 N280 with ADL Enviro400 City 72-seat body, new in 2019. (Tony Wilson)

Reading has bought Scania K270UB gas buses with ADL 42-seat bodies. This 2014 example is leaving Reading railway station in 2018.

Environmental concerns have led to a flurry of alternatives. London operators tended to lead the way; first there were single-deck hydrogen fuel-cell buses in London, and then came hybrid diesel-electric buses that combined a small diesel engine with electric propulsion. The first examples appeared in 2003, and, from 2005, hybrid models from ADL, Optare and Wrights were tested in London service. At the time, hybrid double-deckers proved to be the most attractive option, and substantial deliveries of new hybrid models entered service in London and in many other parts of the UK, starting in 2008.

London operators have tested several alternatives to diesel buses, including hydrogen fuel cell buses like this 2003 Mercedes-Benz 30-seat Citaro O530BZ in 2005, operated by First.

Hybrid diesel-electric buses were a first stage towards pure electrics. Busways Travel used New Zealand-built Designline Olympus hybrids on its Quaylink service linking Newcastle and Gateshead. This 2005 delivery is in Newcastle in 2008.

London fleets were early customers for hybrid models. This 2009 Alexander Dennis 29-seat Enviro200 hybrid is in Kingston when new, working in Transdev's London United fleet.

Optare supplied hybrid Versa models for use on the free MetroShuttle service in Manchester, operated by First, in 2010, like this one in 2013.

Lothian Buses operates Volvo B5LHs with 74-seat Wrights Gemini 3 bodywork; this is a newly delivered 2015 example.

London turned decisively away from new diesel buses to work towards zero emissions. The Volvo B5LH was a popular hybrid model, and this 2016 Go-Ahead London example, here when new, carries Egyptian-built MCV eVoSeti 62-seat bodywork.

The New Routemaster will be recalled as an iconic design that revisited the concept of the modern double-decker. This well-packed 2013 bus running for Metroline demonstrates one of the original advantages of the three-door layout – the open rear platform, a feature subsequently abandoned.

Next came single-deck battery-electrics in 2013; double-deck models followed in 2016. The first hydrogen fuel-cell double-deckers went into service in Aberdeen in 2021, closely followed by the first London examples. Ten earlier Van Hool single-deck models had been tested in Aberdeen by First and Stagecoach between 2015 and 2020.

Right: Another experiment with hydrogen buses was carried out in Aberdeen where Van Hool A330FC 42-seat buses were tried in service with local First and Stagecoach fleets. This Stagecoach example is in 2016.

Below: The UK's first Hydrogen fuel cell double-deckers were built for First Aberdeen in 2020. They are Wrights Hydroliner 65-seaters, as here in 2021. (Keith McGillivray)

Alexander Dennis and the Chinese manufacturer BYD worked together to provide a range of pure electric buses. This Stagecoach South 2018 36-seater, in Kingston in 2021, combines a BYD D8UR chassis with ADL bodywork as the BYD ADL Enviro200EV.

This 2019 Metroline electric Optare MetroDecker MD1050EV 63-seater is one of the growing fleet of electric buses operating in London.

Chinese-built Yutong E12 electric buses have entered service with several UK fleets, including Newport Bus, which operates this 2020 37-seat example. (Sholto Thomas)

Then came the new breed of battery-electric buses – from the Chinese firm BYD (Build Your Dreams), producing complete vehicles, as well as working with ADL, to Caetano, Optare, Wrights and Yutong, plus new entrants to the market including Arrival, Equipmake and Mellor; and Volvo has introduced its BZL with integrated MCV bodywork in single-deck and double-deck forms.

Operators have had to adapt to the new models. Where diesel-engined buses were a known quantity with quick and easy refuelling, the alternative types can be more expensive to buy and require new infrastructure and depots and other premises. Electric buses have high capital costs but a lower energy cost than comparable diesel models; diesel-electric hybrids have lower capital costs and infrastructure requirements, as have biomethane gas buses. Hydrogen fuel-cell buses have much higher capital and infrastructure costs, but, like electric buses, achieve excellent air quality results.

There is now, it seems, everything to play for, and the long-established suppliers to the UK market – ADL, Optare, Scania and Wrights – seem likely to be challenged by newer entrants based both in the UK and throughout the world. However, it is important to recognise how ADL, Volvo and Wrights rose to the challenge with their hybrid models, as well as Scania's concentration on gas models, ADL's partnership with BYD on electric buses, and the reinvigorated Wrights' range of diesel, electric and pioneering hydrogen buses.

Scottish Power has funded small batches of electric seed buses in Scotland, including BYD ADL Enviro400EVs, like this 2021 example working for Lothian Buses in Edinburgh.

Other books you might like:

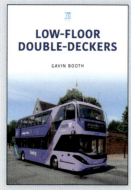

Britain's Buses Series, Vol. 9

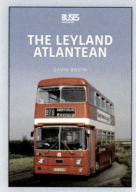

Britain's Buses Series, Vol. 6

Britain's Buses Series, Vol. 5

Transport Systems Series, Vol. 3

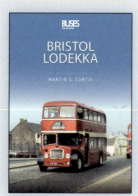

Britain's Buses Series, Vol. 3

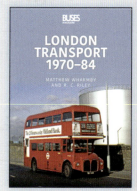

Britain's Buses Series, Vol. 7

For our full range of titles please visit:

shop.keypublishing.com/books